I PUT A SPELL ON YOU

JOHN BURNSIDE

I Put a Spell on You

SEVERAL DIGRESSIONS ON LOVE AND GLAMOUR

JONATHAN CAPE
LONDON

Published by Jonathan Cape 2014

2 4 6 8 10 9 7 5 3 1

Copyright © John Burnside 2014

John Burnside has asserted his right under the Copyright, Designs
and Patents Act 1988 to be identified as the author of this work

This book is a work of non-fiction based on the life, experiences and recollections of the
author. In some cases, names of people, places, dates, sequences or the detail of events
have been changed solely to protect the privacy of others. The author has stated to
the publishers that, except in such respects not affecting the substantial accuracy
of the work, the contents of this book are true.

Lines from *Civilization and its Discontents* by Sigmund Freud are reproduced by permission of
the Marsh Agency on behalf of Sigmund Freud Copyrights and W.W. Norton.
Lines from 'Canto LXXXI' by Ezra Pound, from *The Cantos of Ezra Pound*, copyright © 1948
by Ezra Pound. Reprinted by permission of New Directions Publishing Corp.

First published in Great Britain in 2014 by
Jonathan Cape
Random House, 20 Vauxhall Bridge Road,
London SW1V 2SA

www.randomhouse.co.uk

Addresses for companies within The Random House Group Limited can be found at:
www.randomhouse.co.uk/offices.htm

The Random House Group Limited Reg. No. 954009

A CIP catalogue record for this book
is available from the British Library

ISBN 9780224093873

The Random House Group Limited supports the Forest Stewardship Council® (FSC®), the
leading international forest-certification organisation. Our books carrying the FSC label are
printed on FSC®-certified paper. FSC is the only forest-certification scheme supported by the
leading environmental organisations, including Greenpeace. Our paper procurement policy can
be found at www.randomhouse.co.uk/environment

i.m. Theresa Burnside

The idea, you know, is that the sentimental person thinks things will last – the romantic person has a desperate confidence that they won't.

F. Scott Fitzgerald

My love seems to me like a deep, bottomless abyss, into which I subside deeper and deeper. There is nothing now which could save me from it.

Leopold von Sacher-Masoch

Digressions, incontestably, are the sunshine; they are the life, the soul of reading . . .

Laurence Sterne

CONTENTS

I PUT A SPELL ON YOU

(Nina Simone, 1965)

In the spring of 1958, my family moved from a rat-haunted tenement on King Street to one of the last remaining prefabs in Cowdenbeath, on the very border between the rubble-strewn woods behind Stenhouse Street and the scrubby farmland beyond. It was a move up, in most ways; the prefabs had been built as temporary wartime accommodation but, to my child's mind at least, the cold and the damp, the putty-tainted pools of condensation on winter mornings and the airless heat of August afternoons were minor concerns, compared to the pleasure of living on our own garden plot, in what was, essentially, a detached house, just yards from a stand of high beech trees where tawny owls hunted through the night, their to-and-fro cries so close it seemed they were right there with us, in the tiny bedroom I shared with my sister. Just beyond that stand of trees was Kirk's chicken farm, where the birds ran free in wide pens and Mr Kirk, who lived in an old stone house that I took for a mansion, walked back and forth all day, distributing feed, collecting eggs and mucking out the henhouses. Later, when I was old enough, he would let me walk with him, and I took great pride in keeping pace with a grown man as

1

he went about his business, peering into the incubators and manhandling heavy buckets of grain from here to there, while he watched with contained amusement. On the other side of the house, towards what I liked to think of as open country, the fields ran away to the strip woods in one direction, and the grey, leechy waters of Loch Fitty in the other, and I wandered out there whenever I could, imagining myself a child of the countryside, like the boys in picture books, or one of the chums from the *Rupert* annuals my Auntie Sall gave me every year for Christmas.

I was only three years old when we moved to Blackburn Drive but it wasn't long before I grasped the idea that we really were 'coming up' in the world. By the time I was seven, we actually had a television set and on Sundays, even though it was school the next day, Margaret and I would occasionally be allowed to sit up, eating ice cream from Katy's van and watching *Sunday Night at the London Palladium*. I don't know why I ever thought of this as a treat; the show wasn't very interesting to a seven-year-old and, though they sometimes had pop stars on the bill, it was mostly dancers and novelty acts. Soon, my loyalties switched to *Juke Box Jury*, where you could hear the latest releases and the panellists were slender and nice-looking, with beehive hairdos and mod dresses, like my cousin Madeleine. They weren't as beautiful, though, and when Madeleine came round to our house, as she sometimes did on a Saturday after-noon, I would sit for hours at the kitchen table while she and my mother chatted, fascinated by her long, slim fingers and the cherry-red or powder-blue varnish on her nails. Every time she came, she looked different – new nails, new hair, a new dress – but she was always Madeleine. The very first time we met, at another cousin's wedding, I had fallen in love with her – and I've been in love with her ever since, in various guises. She was ten years older than me and engaged to a merchant seaman called Jackie, but she was the one who led me to understand that the lyrics of all the love songs I'd heard on *Juke Box Jury*, or on my mother's radio, actually *meant* something. I'd thought they were just words, snippets of gibberish and hyperbole that nobody could possibly take seriously; now I knew different because, *now*, I was in love, and love felt very odd, like hearing the first few lines of a story I would never read to the end, because the end belonged to somebody else.

I don't want to pretend that this infatuation was ever a real problem, however. Even my nine-year-old self knew I was suffering from a crush and, besides, there was so much to love back then, in an easy, boyish way that I suspect most men wish would last forever. At nine, I loved almost everything, more or less unconditionally. The hushed theatre of the year's first snow. Teeming thaw water in the ditches and gutters. The arc of a well-thrown ball in the summer sky. That faraway look in Judy Garland's eyes when the dull storyline pauses and she opens her mouth to sing. Kyries and the black vestments on Good Friday. The blur of the host on my tongue and the taunts of the high-school girls as I walked home along Stenhouse Street and up through the woods by Kirk's farm. Most of all, I loved the older sisters of my school friends. Still-slender girls turning into more or less beautiful women and undamaged, for now, by wedlock, they were wonderful, free creatures with money in their purses and sweet, lipsticky smiles for the soppy kid who crossed their paths from time to time. All these things made me happy, and it didn't bother me that such happiness was an affair of the moment. A few minutes, an hour, a September afternoon in the park – the moments came, and then they were gone, so they remained mysterious and uncontaminated: a gift, rather than a burden.

Then, one rainy Saturday afternoon, just after Madeleine and Jackie got married, my mother took me to visit them in their new flat, and Madeleine played us a record she had just bought. It was 'I Put a Spell on You' by Nina Simone and in the space of two and a half minutes I reached the conclusion that this was the most beautiful sound I had ever heard. Everybody stopped talking to listen and, when it was over, we all sat round the table, dumbstruck, until Jackie got up and put it on again. Never having heard the song before, I thought Simone's was the original version and this magical, if slightly sad, afternoon stayed at the back of my mind for years, with the snapshots of my mother and Madeleine in Pittencrieff Park, and the sound of Janice Nicholls on *Thank Your Lucky Stars* saying, 'I'll give it foive,' strands in the fabric of myself that remained more or less dormant, but were there all the same, like the creatures in a fifties horror film, asleep for now in the Black Lagoon, but ready to be reawakened by the smallest shift in the weather or the tide.

I must have heard that song many times, in several versions, over the next decade or so while my father was noisily planning his escape from Cowdenbeath, first via Australia, then Canada and finally, much to my disappointment, by taking a job at the steelworks in Corby, designated a 'New Town' under the 1946 New Towns Act, which had been set up to create 'planned communities' run by the Great and the Good on behalf of the common folk.[1] The move south tore my mother away from her entire family and put an end to my cousin Madeleine's visits, but nobody said anything about that because, according to my father, it was another move up, to a real house, not a prefab, a better job, better schools, better everything. It had to be better, because it had all been planned by professional people who knew what they were doing. In that, at least, I suppose he was right.

Corby was a disappointment in every way, and for my mother it was something close to a personal tragedy. Our 'better house' had three bedrooms, but the kitchen was smaller than the kitchen in our old prefab, and there was no room for a table,

---

[1] New Towns were run, not by the Local Authority, but by an appointed Development Corporation. The Act states: 'For the purposes of the development of each new town the site of which is designated under section one of this Act, the Minister shall by order establish a corporation (hereinafter called a development corporation) consisting of a chairman, a deputy chairman and such number of other members, not exceeding seven, as may be prescribed by the order; and every such corporation shall be a body corporate by such name as may be prescribed by the order, with perpetual succession and a common seal and power to hold land without licence in mortmain.' The chairman at the time Corby was designated was Mr Henry Chisholm, the deputy chairman was the Rt Hon. Lord Douglas of Barloch, KCMG. A history of the Chisholm family notes that Henry was 'knighted in 1971 for his public services, largely from 1950 on for creating and developing Corby, a new town [*sic*]. Henry was widely known and respected in financial and industrial circles for his many interests in several of Britain's companies and industries.'

what with the clunky fitted units. Nevertheless, she put a brave face on it. She went out and bought a new, portable radio and set it on the windowsill, to keep her company, she said, while she baked and cooked, or when she was out in the garden, planting wallflowers. My father had bought a new television too, an ugly cumbersome thing perched on its own stand in a corner of the flock-patterned living room, but the rest of us continued to ignore it and our new home quickly divided along the old fault lines – horse racing and the football results on the goggle-box in one space, *Sing Something Simple* and the new BBC radio stations in another. So I would have heard various covers of 'I Put a Spell on You' over the years, but I didn't pay it any mind till a girl called Annie leaned over the back of her seat and sang it to me one Saturday afternoon in the Charolais cafe, her breath smelling of white rum and instant coffee, her painted smile just inches from my face, her delivery less Nina Simone than a cross between Creedence Clearwater and Arthur Brown, though there might have been a touch of camped-up Janis Joplin in there too. Either way, it was quite a performance.

I was startled by this. I didn't know Annie that well, though I'd often noticed her when she came in, because she was always laughing, always making desperate, slightly hysterical fun of everyone around her, especially herself: a careless, naive, somewhat fearful girl of nineteen, clinging blindly to the sense she had acquired somewhere that, if you didn't take anything too seriously, there would never be anything to worry about.

So I had noticed her, and we'd said hi a few times, but I'd never paid her any obvious attention and I wasn't *attracted* to her, which was always the dividing line, back then, between the girls you bothered with and the ones who blurred into the wallpaper. I did know one of the gang she went around with, a very thin blonde with smudgy blue eyes called Charlotte – and that day, I was aware of her, just off to one side, watching the performance with the rest of the cafe, while Annie carried on singing and I sat frozen, mesmerised by the proximity and the publicness of it all. I'd actually gone out with Charlotte a couple of times, but after a drunken night in Coronation Park it had all come to nothing, and when she started turning up at the Charolais on Saturday afternoons, it came as relief that she had obviously decided to pretend we'd never met. Now, though, she fixed me with a grim, oddly vengeful stare and waited to see what would happen next.

The Charolais was a greasy spoon in Corby's planned community shopping precinct where people from the pubs round about whiled away the afternoon over a coffee or a bowl of ice cream. It was a short walk from most places, and almost next door to my usual Saturday hangout, a dark, faux-timbered bar room called the Corinthian, where you could buy anything from Benzedrine to a cut-price bridesmaid's dress – and this made it doubly convenient because, for a long time, I spent every single Saturday at the Corinthian, right up until the bar staff threw me and the last malingerers out at two forty-five. More often than not, I would be nursing that cup of coffee for hours because I'd spent everything I had by last orders. That didn't matter, though. I didn't go to the Charolais to eat; I went for the company.

Or rather, I was there to wait, with the company, till Karen showed up. Usually, she arrived mid-afternoon, after a trawl round the shops with her friend Kay; because she was married, she didn't sit *with* me, but we had evolved a Byzantine system of signs and prompts that allowed us to communicate back and forth across the room, a system that, nine times out of ten, was effective enough that, when the moment was right, we could slip out and meet somewhere, away from prying eyes. That day, however, she turned up just in time to witness the impromptu serenade and, when Annie broke off suddenly and slumped back into her seat to laugh at her friends, she was the first person I saw among the half-dozen amused specta-tors in my immediate vicinity. She had obviously just stepped through the door and (still, I thought, more or less in role) she was regarding me with what would have seemed, to an indifferent observer, nothing more than amused puzzlement. Yet something else was visible in her eyes and, for a moment, I thought she was hurt, not by some imagined romance with Annie, but by the fact that, because I was single, and a man, I could involve myself in any silliness I liked, while she had to stand by and pretend that she didn't care, not just for her own sake, but also for mine. Her husband, Patrick, was well liked by the Rangers Club heavies and, if our affair was ever discovered, she knew exactly what would happen to us – espe-cially to me. Still, whatever the emotion was that I had seen in her face, it quickly melted away as she nodded briefly, not at me, but at the clutch of girls around the next table, then joined Kay, who had already found a free place some distance away. Kay *knew*, of course, but she had been sworn to secrecy – a secrecy she resented, partly because she thought I was an idiot, but mostly because her husband, Jimmy, was Patrick's best friend and, if things ever came out, she would have some difficult explaining to do. Now and then Kay's intense dislike of me would sometimes come to the surface, and that posed a real threat to our shabby little secret because, as everybody knows, there's a thin line between love and hate and, sometimes, a casual observer will mistake one for the other, with potentially disastrous consequences.

My mother didn't like television to begin with; she preferred to stay in the kitchen and listen to the radio. She would sing along with novelty items from her own era – 'Mares Eat Oats', say, or 'What did Delaware, Boys?' – but when a love song came on, she would stop peeling potatoes or sifting flour, and stand by the window to listen. One favourite, as I recall, was Andy Williams's version of 'Can't Help Falling in Love' – which, in some ways, is the flip side to 'I Put a Spell on You'. To fall willingly, helplessly, under that possibly malevolent spell had, to my child's way of thinking, a troubling innocence to it and, for various reasons, that innocence has beguiled me ever since. Time and time again – helplessly, inevitably – I have rushed in 'Where Angels Fear to Tread' (another Andy Williams favourite) and then, guilty for having made the mistake yet again, I've wondered vainly how to rush back out. Time and time again, I haven't worked out how to deliver the appropriate goodbye and, like my mother, perhaps, I have waited – because, in waiting, there comes a grim satisfaction that while it isn't quite penitence can feel awfully like it.

It's dishonest, of course, this penitential condition. Soon, we who cannot leave our proverbial better halves begin to sneak around, helplessly smitten, or at least diverted, by some passing stranger (though in my mother's case, I am sure, these affairs were purest fantasy, imaginary moments shared with matinee idols,[2] newscasters and, possibly, the odd Catholic priest). The only thing to say in our defence is that we know the other's fear is not of being left by *us*, as such, but of being abandoned, in the abstract, by *anyone*. It's an ashes-in-the-mouth conclusion, when it comes, but it cannot be avoided and, perversely, it offers just that little bit extra to our penitential hearts: for what could be better than a banal and, at bottom, pointless sacrifice? To stay, in effect, not because the other needs me, but because he or she needs *somebody*, and I am better than nothing. It didn't take long to discover that Karen was also a long-standing penitent, the bored wife who would never leave, though she probably prayed every day to be saved by some hypothetical other woman, just as, in the years that followed, I found cause to imagine the perfect other man, a suave, sinister, yet oddly likeable chap who wandered through my daydreams in an Abercrombie & Fitch scarf and Italian shoes, confident and solicitous and ultimately shallow, like some CIA operative (as played by Cliff Robertson) in an old conspiracy movie. I don't know what kind of woman Karen imagined as her rescuer – but I suspect she imagined

---

[2] Her favourite was the tall, handsome Cornell University graduate Franchot Tone, whose marriage to Joan Crawford was one of the reasons for Crawford's lifelong feud with Bette Davis. 'She took him from me,' Davis said later. 'She did it coldly, deliberately and with complete ruthlessness. I have never forgiven her for that and never will.'

someone, and she knew that if this someone didn't come soon, she would never escape.

An hour or so after Annie's serenade, I was in a clearing in the woods behind the Civic Centre, waiting for my secret love. It was one of our special places, and we used it often: there, we could be alone and, should anyone stray from the network of paths that wound between the town centre and the new boating lake, we would hear them coming through the thick undergrowth. As usual, we had left the Charolais separately, taking different routes through town and out, past the swimming baths and the delivery area behind the Civic. I was, as always, the first to arrive and, once she knew the coast was clear, Karen followed. Kay, meanwhile, would be taking a stroll around the shops, providing the basis for whatever alibi might be needed later. It was a matter of principle for us, and perhaps even pride, that we chose to be very careful adulterers, more careful than most in that town – and I don't doubt that we saw ourselves as both guilty and cunning in the conduct of our affair. In truth, however, we were complete innocents.

It was a warm day. Karen always looked her best on warm days; she disliked the cold, hated damp, and thin summer clothes emphasised a figure that I can only describe now, with a mixture of regret and nostalgia, as *lithe*. A slender, rather girlish woman in her mid-twenties, she had light brown hair and amused, searching eyes, but it was her voice I liked best, a sweet, slightly singing voice that, without a hint of affectation, could reduce me to helpless craving whenever she decided to 'talk dirty' (which she did, from time to time, enjoying the effect it had on me a little too obviously). Today, though, she wanted to play another game, a familiar, play-jealousy routine that I never quite knew how to take.

'You want to watch out for Annie James,' she said, as she emerged from the trees and came to stand facing me. 'She's spoken for already.'

I didn't say anything. I just stood watching, waiting to touch her; but Karen had turned unexpectedly serious. She shook her head. 'She's such an idiot, that girl,' she said.

'How so?'

'She's going out with Kenny Wilson now. Which is bad enough. The thing is, Kenny hasn't told Agnes, and when she finds out, it's going to get nasty.'

I racked my brain. I tried to picture this Kenny Wilson, but I couldn't place him, and I didn't know, then, that the Agnes referred to was Agnes McCrorie, a deceptively sweet-faced woman of around thirty who had already built herself something of a reputation. I didn't know either of them and, at the time, I didn't care – what I wanted was the moment, now, with Karen, in the spring sunshine. 'I'm not interested in Annie James,' I said. 'In fact, I'm not interested in anyone but you.' I stepped forward and put my arms around her – and she let herself be gathered in, her body warm and live against me, at once familiar and strange in a way that I could have imagined lasting forever. I touched her face and she tilted her head to be kissed but, as she did, she gave a brief, rueful smile and murmured something that I didn't make out at first. It was only later, when we were getting ready to go, too aware of ourselves and of the possibility of someone stumbling, unexpectedly, into our hiding place, that

I worked out what I'd only half heard and, when I did, the words stayed in my head for hours afterwards.

'But I'm spoken for, too,' she had said. Something like that – and, as with all sinners, she had allowed herself a moment's sympathy for someone who, as unlike her as it was possible to be, was equally smitten and, one way or another, barring some momentous and unlikely good fortune, equally doomed.

I look back now and I see that, as innocent as we were – and as fascinated by the risks we were taking – Karen and I were acting as much from boredom as from romantic or physical attachment. I was a barfly, drifting from one bad deal to the next; she was a more than averagely intelligent factory worker, with a hopelessly disappointing husband and a sense that, while she knew she was too good for Corby, she also suspected that she wasn't good *enough* for anywhere else. Of course, we wouldn't have admitted it then, but we both knew that, having come together as we had, from boredom and disappointment, it was only a matter of time before we grew bored and disappointed with one another, which no doubt explains why, over the next few weeks, I found myself watching for the moment when Annie arrived at the Charolais and, from time to time, in spite of Charlotte's sour presence, I drifted over to her table to make small talk and *be friendly*. I understood that she'd had no special reason for choosing me as the recipient of her voodoo serenade. It had been a piece of theatre and I had just happened to be handy, that particular Saturday afternoon. I knew I wasn't really a character in the story Annie was telling herself about the world – and I don't think, now, that I ever wanted to be – but I couldn't help being drawn to her, because I sensed a mystery in her choice of song. Or, rather, there was something about the way she sang it that went beyond her initial, essentially ironic intent. Her friends had been going on about what Agnes McCrorie might do when she found out Kenny was two-timing her with a teenager, and Annie's song, directed at a random onlooker, was her derisive response – but there was more to it than that. She had only sung a couple of lines, and the first had been harsh and mocking, but something in her voice had softened halfway through the second, so that *I ain't lying* had come out more like a felt melody: wistful, sustained, almost painfully sweet. I imagine that somewhere, in school perhaps, she had discovered the power of the sustained note, and she had obviously sung like this before, for herself more than anyone – to deflect criticism, no doubt, but, at the same time, to reassert some vague hope she had, a hope that, as the songs all begged to know, and in spite of much evidence to the contrary, *love is real*. I wouldn't have been able to put it into words back then, but I see now that *that* was what I was responding to: that hope. All any of us wanted was a chance at something new, something our parents hadn't already failed at. A blind bit of luck. A clean break. A sense that all the fortunate sons, all the better-offs and worthies who planned our communities for us, didn't have what they had because of some natural law which proclaimed, as it carried them along with their many blessings, that we, by contrast, were intrinsically undeserving and, so, justifiably ill-starred.

I heard about the murder on a bright Sunday morning later that spring. It was around ten o'clock and I was on my way to the shops. I had stayed overnight at my sister's house on Station

Road; Karen had planned to sneak out and find me there, but something had gone wrong and she hadn't showed, so now I was trying to cheer myself with the old Sunday-morning routine, fetching orange juice and fresh baked goods and a pile of broadsheets to fill the gap in the day till the pubs opened at noon. I imagine Frank Cronin was doing much the same thing when we met – a lean, rather too matey former school friend with a mop of thin black hair and NHS glasses held together with Sellotape, he was one of those people for whom the unlicensed hours, no matter how well disguised with noisy activity and extravagant carry-outs, had finally become an existential problem. Seeing me outside the Spar shop, he hurried over, glad of a diversion.

'Hey, Dicko,' he said, using an old nickname that still made me wince. 'How's it going?'

'Good,' I said, and he nodded heartily to show that he assumed I was lying. 'What's happening?'

'Not much,' he said, then added, as if it were an afterthought, 'Some girl got stabbed outside her house, down on the Danesholme.' He looked at me. 'You probably know her,' he said. 'Annie James. She's one of Charlotte Walsh's friends.'

'Annie James? When was this?'

'Friday night,' he said. 'So you know her then?'

'What happened?'

Frank gathered himself up, glad to have a small piece of drama to share. 'It was really weird,' he said. 'Some bloke was walking her home and then his ex-girlfriend came out of nowhere with a knife. Just like that. Stabbed her six times, then just stood there screaming at the bloke.' He shook his head. 'Right outside the girl's house, it was,' he said. 'In front of witnesses and everything.'

'So – what happened?' I said. 'Is she all right?'

He stared at me for a moment, as if he suspected this was a trick question, then he shook his head. 'Fuck, no,' he said. 'She bled out. Right on the pavement. Died before the ambulance even got there.'

I stared back. I couldn't quite believe what he was telling me. It was too obvious. Everybody had known something would happen and now it had happened. We stood in silence for a minute or more, turning this thought over in our minds, then I looked at him. 'What did she say?' I asked.

'Sorry?'

'What did she say? The girlfriend?'

Frank began to look troubled at that point, as if he thought he'd maybe said too much. As if the girl he'd told me about mattered to me after all. Though she didn't, of course. She was just a girl from the Charolais. 'She was screaming at the boyfriend,' he said. 'From what I heard, she was saying something like, "You won't want to kiss her now." Something like that.' He thought for a moment, suddenly touched by the story he was telling. 'Fuck me,' he said, apparently saddened and yet, at the same time, faintly impressed by this small detail. 'You won't want to kiss her now,' he said again, shaking his head. 'I *mean*. Fuck me.'

I saw Karen that evening, at the Open Hearth, which wasn't that far from my sister's house. We would go separately, of course, she with Kay and me with a friend I knew I could trust, and we would sit for a while at opposite ends of the lounge, till it felt safe enough to slip outside – me first, then her, always in that order – to talk and fumble with one another in the car park. Sometimes, we would sneak off to my sister's; mostly, though, we plotted our next liaison in the woods, or at her house, when Patrick was on back shift or nights. We had a system for that, too: on certain days, I would walk over to hers and watch for a prearranged signal – lights going on and off in an upper room, the back door left ajar, some object placed conspicuously in a window, it was always changing. When it came, I would let myself in and find her waiting for me in the living room, behind closed curtains. A good deal of planning went into this. On that particular night, however, she found me at the shadowy edge of the car park and, stepping in close, said 'hold me' – and though I knew she was repeating a line she'd heard in an old movie, I also understood that something had scared her. I put my arms around her shoulders and we stood for several minutes in complete silence, not even bothering to check we weren't being watched. Finally, she pulled away and looked up as if she wanted to tell me something. I waited. I assumed it had something to do with the murder, and her sense of a shared doom, but after a moment of trying to find the right words, Karen gave up and turned away. 'What is it?' I said.

'Nothing.'

'You heard what happened – '

She spun round. Light from a nearby street lamp fell on her face. 'Naturally I heard,' she said. 'But that's got nothing to do with us – '

'I'm not saying it has,' I said. 'I just thought . . .' I didn't say any more, because I didn't know what I thought. Or maybe I realised that what I'd thought was trite and unworthy of her.

Karen smiled, then; a wise, all-encompassing smile that was probably half real and half light-effect. 'She was careless,' she said. 'They both were. Careless – and stupid.'

I shook my head. 'It was just bad luck,' I said. 'Nobody could have predicted what would happen.'

She gave a soft laugh and stepped forward slightly, out of the street light, into the shadow. 'You make your own luck,' she said. Then she softened again, and stepped in closer, to lean against me.

I knew I shouldn't say anything, then, but I also knew that *you make your own luck* was enemy wisdom, something the better-offs put about to justify their inappropriate good fortune – and I couldn't help myself. 'And how long does *that* last?' I said.

Karen didn't answer – but I think, at that moment, she realised, perhaps for the first time, that I'd never placed much stock in either the luck or the doom that she lived by – and a month or so later, for no good reason, we stopped seeing one another, drifting apart with a vague sense of having been disappointed, but not quite understanding how.

This far on, I can hardly picture Karen's face at our last meeting, down by the boating lake, when we realised we had nothing left to plan for, but I see Annie James in my mind's eye as if she had died only yesterday – and I can't explain why I am haunted by that particular death. I never really knew Annie, and there are other killings, other ruinations, to commemorate from that time and beyond. Still, almost four decades later, it's this one bad-luck story that stays with me. My sister and a couple of friends from that time still remember Annie as pretty, likeable, somewhat plump, and more than a little silly, but I recall a plain, fairly desperate girl with no distinguishing features other than her bright, overactive eyes – eyes that lit up, that day, when she leaned over the back of her chair in the Charolais and sang a few lines to me from one of Madeleine's favourite songs. No doubt the association has something to do with it – after all, Madeleine was my first real crush, and I still recall the way *her* eyes lit up when the orchestra faded and Nina Simone started to sing. Yet something else is there, too. It's the hint of feverishness in *both* their eyes, the sense I had that they were both as disappointed as I was with the life they had inherited and that they were engaged, moment by moment, in a desperate effort to reinvent the world as they went along. I didn't really know Madeleine – I was too young and too much in awe of her – and I didn't know Annie either, but that doesn't matter. What matters is the story. Annie's wasn't a particularly unusual one, but it was real, because it happened to someone I knew, more or less, and mourned, after she died, for much longer and much more deeply than anyone could have expected. It might sound sentimental to say it in so many words, but we are blessed by the dead, and we know that we are, in spite of our protestations to the contrary. They leave spaces in our lives that, for some of us, are the closest things to sacred we ever know. They are there and then they are gone and, after a time, we come to see a certain elegance in that – the elegance of a magic trick, say, where the conjuror rehearses the vanishing act that we must all accomplish sooner or later.

Nobody in my remaining circle of Charolais acquaintances remembers Agnes McCrorie. This isn't a choice we have made; it's got nothing to do with the tired cliché that the criminal doesn't deserve to be remembered. I suspect that several of these old acquaintances share my there-but-for-the-grace-of-God feeling about such events. In one – and only one – sense, Agnes was luckier than some of us have been: for, even if she doesn't recall much of what happened, she *knows* what her crime was, because it was witnessed and because she was punished for it. There are some for whom that knowledge never comes: we carry on through the half-lit, haunted days with the vague apprehension of some wicked act hanging in the dank tunnels of twenty or thirty years ago, a vague apprehension lit very occasionally by a sudden flash, in which a bloodied face, or a knife blade, or the strange heaviness that comes after brutal violence is almost, but not entirely, illuminated. In some cases, this partial memory is of an act that, strictly speaking, may not be classed as a criminal offence, but the shame involved isn't about illegality; it's about *sin*. I used to believe that the notion of sin was a throwback, something carried forward from Sundays and feast days, when my mother took me to Mass and we implored the pretty lady in the blue headscarf to pray for us, but I don't think like that any more. Now, I think that if anything distinguishes us from the other animals, for better or worse, it is sin. Sin binds us to our fellow sinners, it makes us companionable, and the only people I fear are the ones who believe they are truly innocent, the ones who assume either that they are acting for the greater good of all, or that they can't help themselves.

So, no: it isn't righteousness that erases the killer from my memory, it is the simple fact that, like most killers, she isn't very interesting. And this is where real life and the movies part company: in serial-killer films, even in Agatha Christie, the murderer is a nexus of fascination, often attractive or charismatic, a superior mind or a wilder soul than the other characters in the plot. In *life*, however, he or she is more often than not a dull, even pathetic individual, someone from whom we feel compelled to avert our eyes, quietly and almost automatically, a little ashamed of having looked in the first place and offended, somewhat, by his or her shambling ordinariness. In *life*, if we have souls at all, and if we are able to surrender our presumed innocence, it is the deceased who command our attention, the deceased who are glamoured by the crime, stepping briefly into the spotlight to become more interesting and complex than they ever managed to appear in their beautifully abbreviated lifetimes. It's a bit like that game children play – our version was called Dead Man's Fall – where they pretend to have been shot or blown up and then, in that vivid moment, can see themselves from the outside, more real, more vivid, as if perfected by a sudden flash of lightning while they strike the dying pose and hang beyond luck and doom, before falling into a place where clock time is suspended and anyone might come to grace. It's a necessary game, a child's version of repentance and I wish, as she crumpled and bled away at the gate to her mother's house, that Annie could have played it in her mind's eye, just for a moment, touched by grace and no longer aware of the heat and the noise in the bad-luck story from which she had just been acquitted.

FIRST DIGRESSION: ON *GLAMOURIE*

I put a spell on you. On one level, those are just words, it's all
rhetoric, like every other love song, but on another, those words
hide something beautiful and dangerous and there are times
when I can believe that the singer is capable of some kind of
voodoo magic. In an era of more or less manufactured be-
dazzlement – the shorthand for which is *celebrity* – that sounds
foolish; we are now almost obliged to forget, or to mock, the
old glamourings, the variants of beauty and mania that could
once bewhape[3] and bewilder the soul. Now, almost anyone who
is sufficiently moneyed or pretty or just plain desperate can
become 'a celebrity'[4] and, because celebrity is little more than
the commoditisation of a mask, because its significance is mostly
financial (we think of Daisy, whose voice, Gatsby says, is 'full
of money'), the old link between *glamorous* and *magical* (in the
full sense) has almost disappeared. Nobody cares, now, that the

---

[3] *Verb (transitive archaic). To bewilder; amaze; confuse; utterly confound.* If any
word deserves to be brought back into common parlance, it is this one.

[4] 'When the old gods withdraw, the empty thrones cry out for a successor,
and with good management, or even without management, almost any perish-
able bag of bones may be hoisted into the vacant seat.' (E. R. Dodds: *The
Greeks and the Irrational*)

23

word *glamour* shares its etymology with *grammar* (which formerly meant *any* form of writing: an activity that, in itself, once had an aura of magic to it, especially in societies where most people were still preliterate), or with the French *grimoire*, meaning a book of charms and spells, highly specialised texts that, when performed by the right person, could change the known world.

I put a spell on you. That was, literally, what glamour once did – and the one who cast that spell could be unattractive, imperfect, poor, even repulsive in some way, their power truly mysterious and wholly inexplicable. No gloss, no apparent narrative. Anyone can tell a story, but the writing with which glamouring is associated has nothing to do with such linear or logical matters as plot. Its essence, in the end, is mystery, even bewilderment[5] – which is exactly what the celebrity lacks. Also, with only a few exceptions, it is exactly what consumer culture is clever enough to avoid. When we turn on the TV or the games console, we know that we are about to be *entertained*, and we also know that entertainment is the very opposite of mystery. Suddenly, there is too much light in the house and none of us are children any more, but what does that matter? No point resisting the action hero with his scripted wisecracks, funnier for being what you most expected, just as you know to expect the best-served-cold justice he eventually delivers, as one loose end after another is neatly tied. This justice (i.e. closure) is something you allowed

---

[5] A whole treatise could be written on the etymology of *bewilder*, which shares its roots with wilderness, and originally meant to lead astray, or to lure *into the wild*.

yourself to hanker after through the first hour and a half of the plot, but the moment it comes to pass, you forget about it altogether. True, the movies in which Marlene Dietrich or Louise Brooks put a spell on you also have plots and characters and scripted ironies, but we politely ignore all that. What matters is the moment, or, rather, a series of atmospheres in which the goddess appears, distinct from the entertainment, her mystery intact. Who cares about the script? Who cares about loose ends? When the spell is cast, the script becomes meaningless and we enter into a different contract with the world, into what Old Scots calls *glamourie*, a charmed condition where everything, even the most commonplace of objects or events, is invested with magical possibilities. *Glamourie* is a different way of being in the world, a sudden and sometimes frightening openness, the soul like a door ajar, to paraphrase Emily Dickinson, the physical world immediate and intimate and erotic, invested with new energy and light and, at the same time, beautifully perilous.

Yet, celebrity culture aside, we may all have a *glamourie* hidden away somewhere. It is personal, or at least it seems so, and difficult to disclose. For me, it begins in a ruined house at the end of the Old Perth Road in Cowdenbeath, its windows blind with dust above a lawn that hasn't been cut for years, the interior musty and slightly charred in places, but full of possibilities. A corpse in a cupboard, a live girl buried under the floorboards, dark angels in the rafters: this is my home ground, though it neither belongs to me nor resembles anything I could describe to someone else – which is just as well, for any such thing brought out into the raw light of the public gaze can as easily perish as enchant. This is the inward narrative that is not a story, the scenario that is neither entertaining nor logical – and most of us have the nous to keep it hidden and private, if only because we remember that feeling we had as children, taking out a special object for the nature table, or show and tell, and suddenly being made to see, in the shared light, that the bird's egg, or feather, or mud-caked fossil that had seemed so wonderful in the woods is actually small and insignificant in the workaday world. The child doesn't remember why he loved it before, and the indifference – real or pretend, at that moment it doesn't matter – the obvious boredom of his classmates makes him feel like a traitor, to himself, to the object, and to the entire kingdom of the creaturely and mysterious. Now, he feels hurt and abashed, not just by the coolness of the others, but also by his own feigned detachment – *well, it's nothing really* – and he realises that he has betrayed what should have remained a private matter. At that moment, looking out of himself at the faces of the others, the normal, unglamoured ones, he wishes he had left his chosen object where he'd found it, to vanish into the earth or to melt away in the next big rain.

It comes as no surprise, then, that *glamourie* prefers to remain in the shadows, away from our everyday, rational lives in the ambiguous edgeland that Rickie Lee Jones calls 'the dark end of the fair', a place where anything can happen – though that really does mean *anything*, from a variation on the *Magnum Mysterium* to the most squalid or humiliating of injuries to the spirit. You have to be ready for both, and you go out there thinking you *are* ready, but that's not how the dark end of the fair works; out there you can't really prepare for anything, least of all what you yourself might cause or allow to happen.

Besides, even though the dark end of the fair is a meeting place for the romantic and the perverse, for connoisseurs of pain and the darkest of ascetics, it also attracts the predatory and the parasitical – the soulless ones, the ones who want to translate enchantment and voodoo into hard currency, or those slighted children who are so needy that they have to damage something. What begins by casting a spell can end in aftermath and later, when you go back, just as you went back to the fairgrounds of your childhood to stand gazing at the diesel stains in the grass and the litter on the fence lines – later, when you go back to assuage or confirm your shame, there is nothing to see but a few scratch marks or bloodstains that anybody could explain away in a matter of moments. That's when you begin to understand that you can't go back, you can only repeat – and this is what we do, occasionally for an entire lifetime. We repeat. In the one recurring dream I still have, or at least still remember on waking, I go out in the rain like someone who wants to be somewhere else but doesn't know how to get there. I walk for a while in unfamiliar surroundings and then, suddenly, I know where I am. It's the Old Perth Road of fifty years ago and the empty house is there, the one where everything began. I go to the door, then, and I knock. I am sure somebody is at home, I know, without knowing how, that a fire is burning in the grate and the wild flowers on the kitchen table were gathered fresh that morning, poppies, quaking grass, foxtails. In the dream, I stand a long time, because I know someone is in there, but nobody answers. I knock again, and then again, but nobody ever answers – and that too comes as no surprise.

THE DARK END OF THE STREET

(*James Carr, 1967*)

For years after that wet Saturday afternoon when my glamorous cousin played 'I Put a Spell on You' to my mother and me in her newly rented flat, I thought the song belonged utterly to Nina Simone; thought, not just that she had written it, but that she should have the exclusive right to sing it, for vague reasons to do with womanhood and race and passion, though no doubt the fact that Madeleine loved it so much helped sanctify it in my child's mind. So over the next several years, as each new version appeared in the charts, I felt vaguely offended, even when the cover was a good one. I have no wish to suggest that my teenage self had even the vaguest trace of political sophistication, but I do recall that at least part of the offence, for me, was that, all too often, these covers were issued by more or less likeable, mopheaded and very *white* British Top of the Popsters. I had no idea, then, what authentic was, but the judgemental child in me saw *inauthentic* everywhere. I didn't even appreciate the Animals' version, though usually they could do no wrong ('We've Gotta Get Out of This Place' had become an essential part of the soundtrack loop that ran constantly at the back of my head all through my supposedly formative years, when I knew that I had to escape the world I'd inherited, even if I had no idea how). Still, as concerned with authenticity as I was, it was some time before I learned that Simone's rendition of 'I Put a Spell on You' *wasn't* the original, that the song had been recorded at least as far back as 1957, or possibly even earlier, and not only recorded, but authored by a man called Screamin' Jay Hawkins who, as I came to understand, represented a blackness that was different from and far more ambiguous from than Simone's.

Once again, I really don't want to imply that my teenage self was some kind of political savant or that, in my mostly white, mostly Scottish working-class home town, anyone had very much awareness of race issues beyond TV documentaries and the occasional Sidney Poitier feature, but when I look back I see that, over a period of two or three years, the boy I was came to believe, simplistically, that he was living in a mostly stolen culture. Or if not stolen, then borrowed, sometimes several times over. When I went to discos, I danced with petulant Catholic girls to the Supremes and the Four Tops; alone in my tiny, L-shaped bedroom with my first record player, I listened to music that, while it was sometimes performed by art-school English boys, almost always originated in the Mississippi Delta or the tenements of Southside Chicago. As much as I liked the Stones, I couldn't help feeling an odd thrill of joyous reclamation when Otis Redding came out and sang '(I Can't Get No) Satisfaction' at Monterey, a performance that seemed less cover than cultural salvage. What was best about most English R&B bands was a trail of clues that eventually led to Willie Dixon and Muddy Waters. Behind every white star, a black musician stood in the shadows: Big Mama Thornton, Etta James, Skip James, Willie McTell, Charlie Patton – the list seemed to go on forever, and I was mystified that I couldn't walk into my nearest record store and buy their albums. Not then, at least – and when I came to discover Screamin' Jay, I couldn't buy his records for a long time either.

A stolen culture. It's more complicated than that, I know[6] – and yet it seems significant, even now, that mainstream white audiences found Nina Simone's lush, elegant delivery so much easier than Screamin' Jay's wild, voodoo ranting. Simone may have been radical in her politics and, as a black woman with a strong sense of self-worth, she clearly presented a challenge to the music industry, but she was also a classically trained pianist and a superlative singer who wanted – demanded – to be taken seriously by that mainstream culture and, for many people, 'I Put a Spell on You' is *still* her song and always will be, a curiosity she rescued from the freak show and imbued with restrained passion and taste and recognisable musicianship,

[6] Arguably, the best illustration of this is Wilson Pickett's version of the Beatles' 'Hey Jude'. For two minutes and thirty-five seconds, it's a great cover, but then, two minutes and forty seconds into a four-minute song, Pickett lets rip – and for the next minute and a half, we realise what Paul McCartney was channelling in the original, when *he* lets rip. But there's also a twist to this, because, as Pickett ratchets it up, taking us to a place McCartney could only point towards, he is accompanied by a young *white* session guitarist named Duane Allman, who never stole anything in his life – and, in that minute and a half, we see that, if only we had all shared, nobody would have had to steal anything from anyone. That's why the best photograph in the archives of rock music is of Pickett and Allman, a black superstar and a white session man, laughing together in the studio back in 1968.

turning it into a radio classic that even my mother could appreciate. By contrast, Screamin' Jay had never been blessed (or cursed) with that kind of taste: he was freak show through and through[7] – and that is what makes him a musical genius. For it was his singular, perverse gift that, while he knew how to go about it, he couldn't bring himself to offer the kind of tasteful craftsmanship that a white, middlebrow audience could admire.

I understand that, for many, calling Screamin' Jay a genius is something of a stretch but, having listened to his work for a long time, I don't think it is entirely an exaggeration. What he had was a special form of power, a dark, negative *glamourie* that, even at the end, when all too often he was reduced to self-caricature, could not be entirely concealed.[8] It was glamour in its most baroque[9] form and, like soul, it wasn't a possession or a character attribute, but a visitation, a grace event in which the subject becomes the revelator of some aboriginal narrative that the sane world has forgotten. This crazed grace can lead to moments of extraordinary and recognisable beauty; it can also run into madness, perversity and holy terror – but it is essential to the life of the community. We need the *glamourie*

[7] 'I came into this world black, naked and ugly. And no matter how much I accumulate here, it's a short journey. I will go out of this world black, naked and ugly.' (Screamin' Jay Hawkins)

[8] The title of his 1991 album, *Black Music for White People*, is doubly ironic: mauled by an entertainment business that had no respect for or interest in his real gifts, he was by now parodying his earlier persona, the dangerous, voodoo-Mau-Mau-badman of the fifties.

[9] From the Portuguese *barocco*, meaning a beautifully misshapen pearl.

these creatures offer in order to approximate wholeness; the stories they enact are more vital than logic or money. In the day-to-day world, we allow ourselves to be taken in by cheats and thieves; we are beguiled by money and status; we consume products and celebrities whose only value is assigned to them by advertising and public relations. The beglamoured exist as the antithesis of that world: they give off an other-worldly light that cannot be faked and their visions, no matter how insane or comical, give the lie to the Authorised Version of existence.

There are many reasons why Hawkins the man is an enigma – the most obvious of which is that he exaggerated all the time. What we know about his early life, for example, is mostly speculation and hearsay, with a strong pinch of deliberate obfuscation thrown in for good measure by the man himself. By more or less common agreement, Jalacy Hawkins was born – according to some reports, on a bus – in Cleveland, Ohio, in 1929. Growing up (possibly in the care of an adopted family of Blackfoot Indians) he displayed talents in both music and boxing, winning a Golden Gloves trophy before allegedly going on to become the Alaskan middleweight boxing champion in 1949.[10] When America entered the Second World War he must have been around fourteen years old, but he appears to have joined the

[10] In his 2007 Checkmark-published music guide, *Rhythm and Blues, Rap, and Hip-Hop*, Frank W. Hoffmann states that Hawkins defeated the *future* Alaskan middleweight champion in 1949, before giving up boxing to go into the music business. Hawkins's debut recording was the 1952 single 'Why Did You Waste My Time?', on the Gotham label. He was backed by Tiny Grimes and his Rockin' Highlanders.

army with a forged birth certificate and was quickly shipped out to the Pacific where, by his own account, he was captured by the Japanese and held in a POW camp. Here, the young soldier was tortured by one particular officer repeatedly until – again, by Hawkins's own account – the camp was liberated and he took revenge for months of abuse by taping a hand grenade into the man's mouth and pulling the pin. According to some rumours, he was committed to an insane asylum at the end of the war; at around the same time, however, he would appear to have been studying opera at the Ohio Conservatory of Music. At least some of the biography Hawkins created towards the end of his life is untrue or highly exaggerated (nobody can be in two places at once); still, watching the man tell it, in Nicholas Triandafyllidis's film *I Put a Spell on Me*, it's hard not be taken in by his charm. What is certain is that, some time after the war he began playing piano with Tiny Grimes and Fats Domino (who supposedly fired him for coming onstage in a leopard-skin suit) and by the mid-fifties he had ventured out on his own, signing first with Okeh Records, and then, later, Columbia, where he had his first hit with 'I Put a Spell on You' (though only after some 'noises offensively reminiscent of cannibalistic culture' had been removed).

By that point, Hawkins had created what may well have been the most original, and certainly the most bizarre, stage show in American show business, complete with blazing coffins, Mau Mau and cannibal paraphernalia, live snakes and a cigarette-smoking skull named Henry. At intervals throughout his performances, he would make animal and 'voodoo' noises, call out odd ad libs ('I saw Mau Mau kissing Santa Claus' was a favourite) or set off explosive devices with a wave of the hand; this some-times went badly, and he suffered quite severe burns on more than one occasion. Not surprisingly, the zany act drew the crowds, for a while at least, and he earned high performance fees – which he duly spent on drugs, alcohol and ever more elaborate costumes. Yet his main problem was artistic. Hawkins had a fine baritone voice, and he was a gifted songwriter, but having been backed into a corner by the success of 'I Put a Spell on You' (which would eventually become a Halloween party staple and a jokey soundtrack feature in films like Disney's *Hocus Pocus*), there were times when he was reduced to mugging and self-parody. Novelty acts do not last, no matter how many snakes and skulls they pull out of the bag, and, increasingly, Hawkins's gift was being subsumed by the need to outrage curious fans. A revealing, and rather touching, glimpse of his artistic predicament features on *Black Music for White People*, right at the end of a crazed rendering of 'Ol, Man River' that would have had Paul Robeson turning over in his grave. Screamin' Jay probably knows that he has delivered something extraordinary, but he suspects that this wasn't how it was supposed to go and, after a brief pause, he calls out to someone, presumably the producer: *I got carried away. I got carried away. I think I was doing a live show. I'm sorry. I apologise, I lost my head.* By then, Hawkins had been in the music business for over forty years, so this may have been part of the persona, but that persona had always been a problem, a mix of perverse showmanship and genuine power that really *did* scare the white folks, at least in the early years. The cover of *Black Music for White People* may be firmly tongue-in-cheek, but it also plays with the ambiguity Hawkins engendered in his audience: with animal tusks flaring from his nose and a talismanic horn dangling from his neck, he holds a spear festooned with voodoo charms and a half-decayed skull in his right hand while, over his left arm, a virginal white girl in a pure white lace dress seems to have fainted away from sexual horror, possibly mixed with secret desire. It was all foolishness, of course, but even in 1991 it reminded us of hidden taboos and forbidden pleasures. What Screamin' Jay was offering his audience, what he had been offering all along, wasn't the politicised blackness of a Nina Simone or a Gil Scott-Heron, it was a manic celebration of the dark end of the fair, a serious and playful insistence upon a wilfully perverse and profitless assertion of everything the Authorised Version would expunge from our lives if it could; in short, a gift for, and an allegiance to, the wild that old Scots dialect used to call *thrawn*.

SECOND DIGRESSION: ON *THRAWN*

Even to a native Scot, the word *thrawn* is most readily, perhaps even exclusively, associated with Robert Louis Stevenson's short story, *Thrawn Janet*; which is a pity, because it is a term rich with possibilities that run contrary to the received wisdom of societal norms that, in a wilful and probably futile spirit of opposition, or rather, of refusal,[11] in this digression we will call the *Authorised Version*.[12] I understand that conformity is a complicated matter (of course I do: to be complicated and, therefore, immune to judgement is part of its apparatus), but it would be foolish to imagine that those societal norms are not at least partly there to keep us from rocking our respective planned communities and, in the long run, to maintain a status quo that serves nobody very well, not even the masters of finance and PR who appear to profit by it. It need hardly be said that in most

[11] The distinction being that opposition engages with conventionality on its own terms, while refusal turns aside and looks for new ways to see the world. 'Anarchy is a scientific interpretation of the universe.' (De Bartolomeis)

[12] Freud says it much better, of course, in *Civilization and Its Discontents*: 'Integration in, or adaptation to, a human community appears as a scarcely avoidable condition which must be fulfilled before . . . happiness can be achieved. If it could be done without that condition, it would perhaps be preferable.'

soi-disant enlightened societies (i.e. societies that kill and maim from a distance, rather than close up), the Authorised Version allows for a certain degree of tolerance, in order to maintain an overall balance, a shifting scale of absorption and denial, according to the times and conditions, that is not dissimilar to the precise degree of flexibility, or *give*, engineered into a bridge or a skyscraper that, if it were an entirely rigid structure, would collapse with the first strong wind.

What lies just outside that societal give is what I choose to call *thrawn*, taking my cue from the *Dictionary of the Scots Language*, which translates the word thus: *Twisted, crooked, distorted, misshapen, deformed, awry, turned in a wrong direction. Of people, animals or events: perverse, obstinate, contrary, cross-grained, intractable, not amenable, in a dour, sullen mood.* Of course, in some versions of folk psychology, the word can be used to mean *crazy* or *mad*, but I don't think I am wrong in believing that there is always an element of respect, even of admiration, for the subject so described (unlike such terms as *wuid, gyte* and *daft*, all of which are far less merciful). You can hear it in Scots music, and in the music of Brittany, or Galicia, where the wild whoop, the shriek, the 'barbaric yawp' is highly effective when uttered at exactly the right point in the proceedings, and painfully absurd when it is not (the test is simple: if it makes the hair stand up on the back of your neck, it works; if it doesn't, then it's just for show).

A degree of intractability, of the cross-grained – of an essential and virtuous *wildness* – is a peculiarly Celtic trait, around which turns that most Scottish of spiritual and intellectual enterprises, the so-called 'Caledonian antisyzygy', a term coined by

G. Gregory Smith in his landmark study, *Scottish Literature: Character and Influence*. Smith's claim, in its condensed form, is that Scottish literature 'is remarkably varied, and that it becomes, under the stress of foreign influence, almost a zigzag of contradictions. The antithesis need not, however, disconcert us. Perhaps in the very combination of opposites . . . we have a reflection of the contrasts which the Scot shows at every turn, in his political and ecclesiastical history, in his polemical restlessness, in his adaptability, which is another way of saying that he has made allowance for new conditions, in his practical judgement, which is the admission that two sides of the matter have been considered. If therefore, Scottish history and life are, as an old northern writer said of something else, "varied with a clean contrair spirit," we need not be surprised to find that in his literature the Scot presents two aspects which appear contradictory. Oxymoron was ever the bravest figure, and we must not forget that disorderly order is order after all.'

Disorderly order is order after all . . . Indeed it is, but we may go further and say that disorderly order – that is, the more-than-human order that will sometimes seem disorderly, and even destructive, to us – is the only true and organic order (an implicit, spontaneous, unplanned orderliness we have come to associate with emergence, which is to say, with a new and more generous idea of natural law). In the years since G. Gregory Smith wrote his book (it was published in 1919), we have become aware of Gödel and Heisenberg and 'fuzzy logic', while new translations of the great Taoist texts and the birth of emergence theory have brought us to an understanding that the human idea of order – a woefully stripped-down Authorised Version of events which the best in our midst have always doubted – is an imposition upon nature, and that the true and everlasting (because ever-shifting) order of the world emerges spontaneously out of the workings of the Tao in all things (the Chinese masters called this emergent order *li* and they saw it everywhere. Chu Hsi: 'The term Tao refers to the vast and the great; the term *li* refers to the innumerable vein-like patterns included in the Tao . . . *Li* is like a piece of thread with its strands, or like this basket. One strip goes this way, and the other goes that way. It is also like the grain in bamboo. On the straight it is of one kind and on the transverse it is of another kind.').

What is clear here is that the straight and the transverse, the one way and the other, are both essential for cohesion: in the true order that arises out of the play of *wuji* (primordial being), *thrawn* is not accidental, but the stubborn refusal of an imposed, Authorised Version of things that quite simply does not work. The political ramifications are clear: 'Either the State for ever, crushing individual and local life, taking over in all fields of human activity, bringing with it its wars and its domestic strug-gles for power, its palace revolutions which only replace one tyrant by another . . . *or* . . . the destruction of States, and new life starting again in thousands of centres, on the principle of the lively initiative of the individual and groups and that of free agreement. The choice lies with you!' (Peter Kropotkin, *The State*). It is clear that to be *thrawn* is already to take a first step towards shrugging off the State in all its manifestations and so to commence working for the spontaneous expression of individual and local life – not an easy matter, as there is so much socialisation and Authorised Version garbage to *unlearn* before the *vita nuova* can begin. So much to root out that was seeded in us as defenceless children – all that guilt and obedience and weakness we were taught over our father's knee and in primary school. Surely it is to this learned set of limits and blames that Blake is referring when he speaks of 'mental fight'; and if *anyone* is to be free (I hope it goes without saying that no one can be truly free until freedom is universal), then *everyone* must learn, from leaves and wild flowers and grains of sand, that true order is not imposed, that communities are not *planned* and that human designs are successful only insofar as they emerge from a conversation with the natural. Which is not to say that we must search for order in the world around us; on the contrary, the task is to prepare ourselves to see *without* seeking, to *be with* the world as it happens, rather than trying to control and enumerate it. When we do that, we see the true value of all that is *thrawn*.

Of course, if we return to that dictionary definition we find some seemingly negative or pejorative interpretations of the condition. *Contrary*, for example; not to mention *cross-grained, intractable, not amenable, in a dour, sullen mood.* It would seem at first acquaintance that qualities such as these have no virtue at all, but there are certain occasions – certain weathers – when the stubborn, the dour and the cross-grained, like the remorseless optimist or the fool, work for the common good. We remember, for example, how Gurdjieff liked to have a contrary spirit among his followers. One individual who joined his group was always complaining and unsettling the other students to such an extent that most of them were relieved when that man threw down his gardening tools, hurled insults at the Master, and lit out for Paris; but Gurdjieff took the trouble to go after the apostate and, after much persuasion, brought him back. The explanation he gave for this seemingly foolish act was that the man's cross-grained, argumentative temperament – his *thrawnness* – kept everyone around him from falling into lazy mental routines and an easy mysticism that might prevent them from achieving the awakened state they had come to Gurdjieff to find.

Another example of *thrawn*'s none too obvious virtues can be drawn from the teachings of the Taoist sage, Chuangtse (Chuang Tzu) who, when Hui Tzu compared him to an old and twisted Ailanthus (known to us as the Tree of Heaven, but to the Chinese as *chouchun*, the stinking, or foul-smelling tree), responded that such a tree had many uses. True, it was of no practical use to carpenters or builders, but it offered shelter for meditation, and shade from the noon sun – and it was an instance of the wild spirit that is much prized in Taoist gardens. Thus, because it was of no obvious use to others, it would endure, both as a lasting reminder of that wildness and as a symbol of the *thrawn* spirit's key attribute of non-action, or *wu-wei*, (coincidentally, with its active medicinal constitutents mersosin, tannin and amarolide, the bark of this tree is also used in Chinese herbal medicine, for example as a cancer treatment).

There is real virtue, then, in being of no use; real virtue – and longevity, too, a point that would not be lost on Chuang Tzu's readership, who were only too aware of the perils of being useful, for a time, at the emperor's court. In Chuang Tzu's philosophy, there is much to learn from the useless (and so, ungovernable), for, as this old anarchist insisted, the world 'does not need governing; in fact it should not be governed', while maintaining, as a central pillar of his teachings, the principle of *wu-wei,* usually translated as 'doing by not doing' (a practice that should not, under any circumstance, be confused with that old hippie notion of 'going with the flow'. To practise *wu-wei,* we have to study closely how the flow works and learn, not so much how to help it along, as how to prevent ourselves from getting in its way). An essential element of Chuang Tzu's teaching is that we lose our sense of order – or meaning, or happiness – when we go looking for it because, almost inevitably, we only find what we expect to discover and not what is actually there. This is the result of conditioning – of growing up socialised, straight and true, sane, adjusted, a good egg, a pillar of the community. We don't dare to admit that we've begun to suspect that the Good we were taught to seek is a contrivance to keep us in place and, as a mother will say of a well-behaved child, *no trouble.* The trouble is, we need trouble: we need the seemingly disordered, the *barocco,* the *thrawn.* We need the true alternative to the Authorised Version, which is not just protest or rebellion, but an actual, out-and-out refusal to allow the societal to become our be-all and end-all.

What this refusal entails is the giving up of a certain kind of belonging – that is to say, of the apparent belonging of possession. For the not-*thrawn,* all belonging has to do with possession: from the daily business of self-possession, which is to say a closing of the mind and the nervous system to ensure that the ghosts and the earth gods are excluded, to every form of control exercised over the lives of others, a control that is as much exercised in a certain way of looking as in overt tyranny or violence. For the *thrawn*, such possession is the very antithesis of belonging – is nothing more, in fact, than a routine enactment of *being present* in which attentiveness is sacrificed for an illusion of ownership. For the self-possessed, *thrawn* is an embarrassment, or an inconvenience; they do not see its virtues, as Chuang Tzu did, and they are unable to appreciate that *Thrawn Janet* is touched, not just by a kind of madness – that is, the shrugging off of self-possession – but also by an eerie inward light, and by a secret understanding that, while it may never be articulated, can be seen at work in the eyes of the rapt, the inebriated and the mad. At its keenest, *thrawn* reminds me that there is always a gap between the inward life and the outward appearance and so, essentially, that the subjectivity of every other is signally different from my own – and *that* casts the entire societal order into doubt. Fresh from an encounter with the *thrawn*, I begin to see that the societal *you* is as much a pretence, as much a mask, as the societal *I* – and I am glad. We may never abandon this pretence, but it is good enough just to know that a pretence is a pretence, a mask is a mask, and there is, or may be, something indelible behind that show. This is why we should count ourselves fortunate when we discover *thrawnness* in our companions and neighbours, for they are a manifestation of the wild right here in our midst, where they are totally unwarranted and, for that very reason, should be made all the more welcome. Disorderly order, the beauty of the useless, the value of contrariness, the joyful project of refusal: these are urgent matters for us now, in a world where even to desire the wonderful – which always and of necessity has its wild component – is seen as an aberration. All around us, officials of the Authorised Version take it upon themselves to parcel out the real as a marketable commodity and, out of sheer gall and not much else, would have us believe that the whole world belongs to them. Yet nothing could be further from the truth – and the *thrawn* are a constant reminder of that. If reality belongs to anyone, it belongs to those who refuse to possess it. That is the paradox, always. Without wild there is no order; without perversity, nothing is pure; and without the misshapen beauty and unaccountable grace of *thrawn*, proportion, in any form, is impossible.

YOU CAN'T DO THAT

(The Beatles, 1967)

For a long time, whenever anyone enquired about my religion, I would say, in a resigned tone, that I was born a Catholic, and it was only recently that I took notice of the fact that this wasn't quite right. I was born an unsocialised, neutral creature, a near *tabula rasa* with a few lines of rather unprepossessing genetic graffiti scrawled in the margins, and for the first four years of my life I lived a privileged, near-pagan existence, confined to the backyards and drying greens of various tenements, my only deities spiders and blackbirds and the Halloween shadows that took form and melted away moment by moment on the walls of the communal wash houses. That first world was a sovereign realm of women – my mother, my aunts, our female neighbours – which meant it was mostly happy, in an offhand way. Those women were poor, ill-educated for the most part, and often Byzantine in their codes and superstitions, but they were still women, which meant that, when the men were absent, they could smile or laugh for no obvious reason and, unlike the men I encountered, mostly at family occasions, they were capable of being calm, rather than merely still. I went to church in those preschool years, of course, but I remained untouched by dogma, my awareness tinted by the scents and colours, the flowers on the altar and the various blues of Our Lady's painted vestments, but directed for the most part at my aunts and female cousins, utterly transformed and glamoured by their Sunday best. Fewer men than women went to Mass; my father was rarely present, but when he did come, he looked awkward and out of place, like the other working men who stood mouthing, but not actually uttering, the hymns and responses for that day's order of service – and for a time, all these giants of my world looked small, bemused and diminished by a ritual that, as tedious and silly as it was, not only stood between them and any afterlife they might wish to imagine, but also privileged the pious womenfolk over whom, on any other day but the Sabbath, they would have towered, superior in muscle and, invariably, in that Scottish pit town, in earning power. Yet the real reason for their awkwardness was the fact of the priest, a man so adamantly on the side of the women and children that he seemed not a man at all, but a chimera in vestments, a soft-faced ventriloquist's dummy who was always right because everything he said was pre-authorised and institutional, part of the fabric of the social order, and so beyond question. Even worse than this, however, was the priest's trump card: his celibacy. That God's representative on earth was so fiercely asexual was a signal that nobody could ignore and, while the men stayed away as often as they could, the women placed their trust in, and retained their deepest admiration for, a creature whose presence in their midst was a living repudiation of sexual desire.

*   *   *

Like most boys, I was forced, if not entirely to give up, then at least to downplay my infant loyalty to the pagan world as soon as I began attending school. That also entailed the surrender, or at least the dutiful concealment, of certain erotic pleasures that were natural to that world. Licence to touch and to smell as I liked, the freedom to put a bird's egg in my mouth and savour the warmth of it, an unhesitating, infantile curiosity about bodies and matter, musts, sediments, stains, vapours, bodily fluids. By the time I started on the innocent courtships approved by my betters, I was the very model of a good Catholic boy – and the girls in my circle were all unrelentingly good too, which meant they didn't smell, they didn't have bodily fluids and they kept their starched white knickers on at all times. People said that, for 6*d*, a girl from the Prod school called Junie Dee would take you to a secret place of her choosing, lift her skirt and show you what was underneath and if you gave her a shilling she would let you slip your index finger inside, but I never took advantage of this service, not so much out of loyalty to *Sacra Virginitas*,[13] as the need to preserve my sixpences and shillings

[13] Virginity fully deserves the name of angelic virtue, which St Cyprian writing to virgins affirms: 'What we are to be, you have already commenced to be. You already possess in this world the glory of the resurrection; you pass through the world without suffering its contagion. In preserving virgin chastity, you are the equals of the angels of God.' To souls, restless for a purer life or inflamed with the desire to possess the kingdom of heaven, virginity offers itself as 'a pearl of great price', for which one 'sells all that he has, and buys it'. Married people and even those who are captives of vice, at the contact of virgin souls, often admire the splendour of their transparent purity, and

for the pictures, where I fell in love with a different actress every week, with no concern as to type – Lee Remick, Vanessa Redgrave, Jean Hale, it was all the same to me. Compared to them, the women in my immediate circle seemed incomplete, like unfinished cartoons – until, on an ordinary weekday outside the newsagent's on Greenhill Rise, everything changed.

I had a paper round in those days. Obviously, I only did it for the money and, to begin with, all I noticed was how long it took, and how heavy the bag was when I set out, a dead weight dragging me down as I trudged from one street to the next, the houses dark, the gardens still, my footsteps echoing into cul-de-sacs and out again, a bleak and, at the same time, oddly comforting sound. For the first week or so, this paper round was nothing more than a chore, something I did to get money for records and comic books, but after a while, when I became accustomed to the weight of the bag and eventually learned how to pace myself, I began to feel that the time I spent trudging around the Beanfield Estate was the best part of my day, a clear and quiet interim between the fug of home and the futile riot of school. I loved the sweet, cool smell at the edge of the woods and the birds singing to the orange street lamps on Gainsborough Road – and I loved the moment, towards the end of the round, when those street lamps were extinguished, all at once, and everything went dim and silky, while my eyes adjusted to the

feel themselves moved to rise above the pleasures of sense. (*The Encyclical of Pope Pius XII, On Consecrated Virginity,* 25 May 1954) plain light of early morning. I would drop my bag off at the shop, lingering a while in the warm, surprisingly golden interior, unwilling to go back to the usual day and ever so slightly intoxicated by the smell of newsprint and the brightly coloured adverts for soft drinks or fireworks; then, reluctantly, I would head for home, the houses lighting up on Farmstead Road and Ashurst Crescent as I passed them by. People would come to the windows to draw the curtains, hatchet-faced women weary of marriage and factory work, uniformed girls from Our Lady's or the Grammar, and I would feel too visible, too much in the open, when their eyes picked me out from the gloom, as if I were an animal that had strayed from the woods and into the middle of town, where it didn't belong.

One day, I got back early from my round. It was a spring morning, crocus time and still cold, but the air smelled of fresh rain and budburst and, from the first, my sack had seemed less burdensome as I walked rather than trudged around the estate, head up and alert for the meaner dogs I occasionally met on that route, yet blessed by the seemliness of gravity and more awake to my surroundings than I had been when I set out – and that, no doubt, was why I noticed the tall, dark-haired woman who was coming out of the shop just as I was going in, my empty sack hanging off my shoulder, my heart lighter than usual. It is possible that I had encountered this woman before but, if so, I could not have seen her face because, as I passed her by in the old-gold light of the shop's interior, I became aware of an entirely new branch of logic suddenly at work in the universe. At the same time, however, I noticed the fine, ridged scar that ran from just below her right ear and down her neck – how much further it went I couldn't tell, because she was wearing a thick sweater under her raincoat, and I had to look away when she saw that I was staring at her, even though, in the millisecond before I turned my head, I was given to understand, by the faint smile that flickered across her face, that she had taken that stare as a compliment, a homage to her beauty, rather than a child's morbid interest in her disfigurement. That crossing of our paths lasted only a moment, and before I could do or say anything, she was gone. Over the next several days, and then weeks, I paced my paper round to the nearest minute, so I would be back in the shop at the exact same time every morning, but I never saw her again. I asked the newsagent several times if he knew her, but he didn't even remember who I was talking about and, in the end, he got tired of my questioning. It was a long time before I finally acknowledged she was lost and, when I did, I was desolate for weeks; but on that first day, I stopped being haunted by Lee Remick and all those other improbable Hollywood beauties I had secretly lusted after. Now, my deepest allegiance was to a different form of beauty. I still went to school dances and the Catholic Club disco, and I had (mostly) normal, more or less pretty girlfriends, after a fashion, but what I really wanted was a romance that, at that time, I couldn't have put into words, but could picture in my mind's eye from a photograph I had once seen, an early sepiatone portrait of a naked dancer in what looked like a rough, hessian mask, a mask that she was obliged to wear to cover a beauty, or a disfigurement, so intense that it could only be guessed at, never shown. In short, I had begun to want the impossible and to settle for anything less struck me as both cowardly and a touch insulting to the Beloved.

EVERLASTING LOVE

(*Love Affair, 1967*)

If we are to believe Dante, love moves the sun and the stars (*'l'amor che move il sole e l'altre stele'*);[14] Sappho compared it to a mountain wind, and Aristotle believed it came about when a single soul inhabits two bodies, but back in the real world, I was more inclined to go with songs like 'Let's Spend the Night Together' (the Rolling Stones, double A-side with 'Ruby Tuesday', 1967), or 'Somebody to Love' (the Great Society, 1966; Jefferson Airplane, 1967). It was sex that mattered to my fifteen-year-old self, even if I tended to gloss it as love. As Grace Slick said, in response to the Beatles' first US chart-topper, 'Of course you don't wanna hold her hand, you wanna dick her!' In my mid-teens, I persuaded myself that I was in love, on average, about five or six times a week – with my mother's friend Beryl, say, or the Pinta Girl, or the actress who played Doctor Who's assistant, Zoe; but love, in any scenario I dared to imagine, was mostly just code for desire. Mostly. The one drawback was that my ideas about such things had been formed by radio – my mother's radio, in fact, which, for the first twelve years of my life, was permanently tuned to the unending

---

[14] *Paradiso*: Canto XXXIII.

sentimental education provided by *Pick of the Pops* and *Sing Something Simple* on the BBC Light Programme. Here, sex was rarely, if ever, mentioned. It was always *love*.

Listening to the radio wasn't a lifestyle choice. It was a declaration of loyalty. As noted, the TV sat in what we had recently started calling 'the lounge', and was used mostly by my father; my mother spent very little time in that room, at least when he was at home. She would clean it, and keep it tidy and, in the winter, she would get up at six and make a fire, but her true domain was still the kitchen, where she lived like a ghost from the 1950s with what she still called 'the wireless' – and, because everything that was real in our lives happened in the kitchen, it was radio that provided the white noise and the soundtrack to my daily round, a constant wash of mostly vintage love songs, all *never let me go*, and *you belong to me* and, worst of all, *I don't have anything, since I don't have you* . . . My mother knew most of them by heart: 'You're All the World to Me'; 'Can't Help Falling in Love' (the Perry Como version, not Elvis); 'Love is a Many-Splendored Thing' (I didn't even know what that meant – what the hell was many-splendored? When I asked her about it, she laughed, but there was a darkness behind her laughter – a darkness, or a sadness; I was too young, which is to say, too self-involved, to tell).

At that age, I didn't know that she was hanging on to a fantasy that she couldn't do without, a fantasy, not that the many-splendored love her marriage so clearly lacked existed out there somewhere, but that, underneath it all, behind all the fights about money and the tears and the abuse, she and my father still loved one another as they had in the beginning (a time she never spoke about, oddly enough, though he would, when the mood was on him: how they met, the presents he brought back from his RAF postings, their honeymoon in Aberdeen, of all places). *In extremis,* he would even grow maudlin about it all, declaring that he'd never loved any woman but her, though he'd had every chance back in his RAF days, and even now, the women down at the club were throwing themselves at him. Those sentimental nights provided us kids with a sorry spectacle that my mother never stayed up to see, yet in spite of all this, in spite of the fact that she had every reason to feel bitter, or to have dismissed the whole many-splendored thing long ago, she could still be brought to a halt, in the middle of cooking, or a Saturday baking session, by some old favourite with lyrics that, in any explicable world, would have stuck in her craw. She would stand by a window, or over the cooker, ladle poised above the split-pea soup, singing along – she had a thin, but oddly sweet voice – and it didn't matter if I rolled my eyes, she just went on singing, a true believer, if not on the workaday level, then at least in the abstract.

It was all mighty peculiar, as our neighbour, Jim, used to say and it left me mightily confused. On the one hand, the impulse to mock this nonsense was both natural and pressing – and yet, at the same time, there was a sense that something real was concealed behind it all, something that, if it were allowed to sour, would leave a gap, not just in my mother's, but in all our lives, an emptiness that nothing else could possibly fill. Where we lived, everything was cooked in lard, white pudding was a Saturday-night treat, the men all smoked eighty a day and drank themselves into oblivion every chance they got, but the real killer, the thing that truly sapped your strength, like a leech sapping the blood from your heart, was disappointment (synonyms: failure, defeat, frustration), a word whose etymology – from Middle French *desappointer*, 'to undo an appointment, to remove from office', – barely hints at its destructive power, but, given a moment's further analysis, does express something of the pain of workaday defeat that people in that world endured. If a soppy love song could ease that sense of defeat for a while, who was I to mock? The fact that, on occasion, during my clever-clogs years, I *did* mock now shames me more than I can say.

The older I get, the happier my childhood becomes. I still know about the times when my father got drunk and came home covered in blood ('bleeding like a sheep', he'd say, beglamoured by the reek and the heat of it), the nights when I had to climb out of the window to escape his drunken rages, the hours of waiting, wondering where he was, and whether he'd spent *all* the money: I know this, but I don't *feel* it now the way I *feel* those Saturday afternoons in our various kitchens, the table or fitted counter sheeted in flour and three trays of fairy cakes in the oven, the back door open to let out the steam, blackbirds singing in the neighbour's lilac tree and Andy Williams on the radio singing 'Can't Get Used to Losing You'. When the Beatles stopped being lovable mop-tops and went all Sgt Pepper, I started to get sniffy about *Sing Something Simple* with its opening tagline – *We invite you to Sing Something Simple, a collection of favourite songs, old and new, sung by the Adams Singers, accompanied by Jack Emblow* – and I was pleased with myself, whenever I managed to bite my tongue. I was fine with 'Can't Get Used to Losing You' just as long as I didn't listen to the words – the trouble was, my mother couldn't hear the opening bars of a song she knew without joining in, usually sotto voce, it has to be said, but it was still enough to make me aware of the sentiments being expressed, and the irony of the situation, given the *whole life through* part. On the radio, love was a many-splendored thing, but the marriages I was privy to seemed more like war zones.[15] I don't want to suggest that matrimony was *necessarily* a tragic affair – some of our neighbours' marriages seemed quite functional, if somewhat routine; nevertheless, in the workaday world, it is wedlock that is most likely to offer the occasion for life-threatening disappointment. Wedlock, or parenthood – and, when it's not caused by poverty or ill health, most of the misery inflicted by parents is a result of their marital unhappiness. Growing up, I blamed my father for everything, overlooking his very obvious wretchedness, and it wasn't until much later that I began to wonder what wedlock had cost *him*, married as he was to a dutiful and sexually repressed Catholic of a certain class and generation. I cannot rule out the idea, now, that he could have been a painfully frustrated sensualist, a husband cheated of what might have been the only means he had to express his love; his passions, his inner boy's desire for joy and sex curdling into violent frustration. That frustration might not have been the sole cause of his drinking and gambling, but it's not very surprising that he should take refuge in the sins he knew to escape the shameful and ugly desires that had once seemed the most natural thing in the world (within marriage, of course). It needn't have been so ugly, or shameful,

---

[15] 'Marriage is like life – it is a field of battle, not a bed of roses.' (Robert Louis Stevenson, *Virginibus Puerisque*)

either. That's an assumption that's too often made about men when, in truth, the porno mentality isn't native at all, it's conditioned in. Wherever my father ended up in his mind or in his spirit, it may be that, to begin with, the poor man just wanted to *play*. Maybe they both did, but they couldn't quite elude the stare of the little yellow-eyed, jaundiced god that had been implanted at the back of their minds. I remember, once, much later, I found a stack of dirty magazines hidden in his wardrobe while I was searching for a tie to borrow and he came in just as I picked up a copy of *Knave* from the top of the pile. He didn't say anything then, he just turned round and went back downstairs to the 3.15 at Chepstow or whatever, but that evening, in the Hazel Tree, where we used to go to play crib, father and son together, he told me quietly not to take any notice, he never read that stuff, it was just something a mate from work had passed on – and I believed him, immediately and without reservation, because, when it comes to that kind of thing, what's to read? Besides, for a moment there, it all seemed to balance out: they had both been cheated, not just by the class system, as such, but also by the sexless, loveless moral apparatus that, as I grew up, I increasingly came to think of as societal, an apparatus that existed for no other reason than to stifle in its subjects any sensual pleasure and any kind of sex, other than the plastic-fantastic couplings of porn, or the bowdlerised, abstract crooning of Tin Pan Alley.

No surprise, then, that, as we took the floor at the Catholic Club disco or the end-of-term dance, we didn't hear any songs that talked about the slow attrition of mistaken commitment. Songs where the heart resembles nothing so much as a knob of lard tossed into a skillet and skittering around on the hot steel, squeaking and fizzing as it gradually diminishes to nothing. That was what everlasting love meant to me, before I even got on to the dance floor. It was a pose, an attitude – and I wanted nothing to do with it.

Fat chance of that.

Lovers, to bed; 'tis almost fairy time.

Sometimes, though only in my most unguarded moments, I can still think of Annette Winters as my first love. At fifteen, she was tall, slender, very dark, an intelligent, sly girl possessed of what I think of now, though I didn't think of then, as a kind of debatable beauty. She refused to be pretty in the ordinary sense that made girls *attractive* in our neck of the woods, but the main thing that drew me to her was that she did what she wanted, come hell or high water, and that was rare. In the town where we grew up, the will of girls and women was continually sapped, from cradle to crone, boyfriends and husbands taking over where parents left off, but so far Annette had come through with all her faculties intact. Maybe it wasn't love so much as admiration that drew me to her, but I *was* drawn – and there were times when she was drawn to me too, though if what happened between us could even be described as a relationship, it was very much of the on–off variety. When it was on, we spent hours lying around on my bed or her parents' floor transforming endless foreplay into a form of torture (there being no after to this fore, so to speak: Annette was, after all, a good Catholic girl); when it was off, it was because *she* had suddenly remembered that *I* wasn't her type.

Not being her type included a wide variety of faults, from having light brown hair to being 'bookish', features that I thought neither here nor there. In fact, the whole 'type' thing was just so much nonsense, in my enlightened fifteen-year-old view. It might have been interesting at another level, where it really told you something about a person. For example: is your type the pretty, loyal 'secretary' who is always in the background in old American detective movies, or the mysterious, but slightly *too* existential woman who turns up in his office unannounced and will, almost inevitably, betray him in the final reel? Though, come to think of it, that doesn't help much either: I usually fell for the hat-check girl you only see in passing when the detective drops by the fat man's nightclub to give him the once-over, or maybe the femme fatale's younger sister, excluded from the grown-up stuff and left to sulk by the pool in her swimsuit or her immaculate tennis whites. Whenever Annette went off on one of her not-my-type deals, I would sit in the town library compiling questionnaires like the ones that used to appear in newspapers and women's magazines.

What's Your Type?

Answer these ten questions to find out if the girl you're with is really the one for you . . .

1. You are invited to meet one cast member from *Pal Joey*.
   Who do you choose? Is it:
   a) Rita Hayworth?   b) Kim Novak?   c) Frank Sinatra?

2. The girl you're with has a new hobby. Is it:
a) Playing the piano   b) Hill-walking   c) Ikebana

Etc. It's pitiful, the depths to which we sink when abandoned.
At fifteen, I didn't know much about much, but I did know
that the only one thing worse than endless foreplay is no foreplay
at all.

Still, the 'not-my-type' concept did have some merits. Anyone
who frequented Our Lady's Catholic Club disco back in the late
1960s will no doubt recall the time when Grace Noonan was
dragged into the hall by her maternal grandmother, an ur-crone
of a woman universally known as Ma Keane. Nobody could have
missed their dramatic entrance, but then nobody with any sense
would have got in Ma's way, as she climbed up on to the stage
and carefully lifted the stylus from the 45 single DJ Stu Bonham
had just started to play (I remember it now: it was in fact the
original version of 'Everlasting Love', by Robert Knight. Not
the Love Affair version, you understand, but the original. Stu
Bonham was something of a purist in such things). Now, he
looked on in awe and wonder as the old woman – a cross between
Cruella de Vil and the old Irish biddy who, in John Ford's *The
Quiet Man*, offers John Wayne a 'good stick to beat the lovely
lady' – called for hush. Not that there was any need: a fascinated
silence had fallen on the dance floor and somebody had even
switched on the lights nearest the stage. Standing beside her aged
relative, Grace, who would have been fourteen at the time, looked
wonderfully defiant, staring out curiously at the sea of faces as
if her grandmother wasn't even there.

'Some of you know our Grace,' Ma Keane cried, her voice

hoarse from centuries of Benson & Hedges Gold. 'She's not fifteen yet, but some gobshite in this room has got her pregnant anyway.'

A soft gasp of embarrassment flickered through the crowd, followed by the distinct sound of suppressed tittering.

'Aye, yez can laugh all ye like,' Ma Keane roared. 'But when I find out who it was, I'll cut his balls off . . .'

Now, for the first time, Grace looked at her. 'Ye will nut,' she said, with admirable contempt.

'Ah feckin will,' the old woman retorted, turning again to the crowd. 'Come on, youse,' she said. 'Who is it? It has to be somebody here.'

At this, several of the lads at the back of the hall, the ones who flitted to and fro between the dance floor and the boys' toilets to sip on carefully concealed cans of Special Brew, burst into laughter, at which another lad, a smooth-faced carrot-heid called Kenny Lavin, shouted, 'Hey, Ma, yer watter's bilin,' which set the whole crowd off.

We had to give Ma Keane her due, though; she wasn't going to be beaten that easily. With the DJ's mike in her hand, she lurched to the front of the stage, and leaned into the crowd. 'Has nane of yez got a shred of honour or decency in ye?' she said, her voice wonderfully pitched between total contempt and a puir auld woman's sadness at the way of a world she'd had to endure for far too long. 'Somebody here knows who the bastard is. Make him do the right thing and stand by this wee lassie.'

'Why don't you ask her?' Kenny Lavin called, at which somebody further back added a stage-muttered, 'There's a fair few to choose fae.'

For a moment, Ma Keane's face softened and, for that instant, it looked as if this farce might turn into something akin to tragedy. 'Why dae ye think I'm here?' she said. 'The girl won't give us a name.' She looked back at Grace, who had now succumbed to the embarrassment of it all and was staring off to the left. It looked to me that she was on the edge of tears. Ma Keane turned back to stare down at those of us who were gathered close to the stage. 'She's no saying,' she said – and we all shuffled and looked at our feet, ashamed for her, and for Grace, and for whosoever the father might be. Not that anybody though he should give himself up and go willingly to the fate that we, or we boys at least, might know was coming to us, but still hoped to avoid. What that guilty boy was supposed to do was step up and marry Grace; which was fine in principle, but we had all seen enough of our parents' lives to feel that marriage was a trap[16] constructed, not by women and girls, but by 'The System' to keep us in order. That was the term we used as a kind of shorthand for a job at the Works and your name on the housing list and the ubiquitous conspiracy against human wildness – *The System* – and if you lived in that town, or anywhere like it, it was hard not to think that this shorthand was fair, based on the evidence. The pleasures of married life weren't too visible in Corby in the early 70s and, even if you weren't the political type, it was clear that marriage – and parenthood – tied people to a life that suited the bosses. The

[16] 'Times are changed with him who marries; there are no more by-path meadows, where you may innocently linger, but the road lies long and straight and dusty to the grave.' (Robert Louis Stevenson)

joy of being a parent wasn't much in evidence either: what kids saw, growing up, was the worry, the strain, the sad business of not having enough money for the televised Christmas ideal, and the shame of not being able to say so. But there was one difference between boys and girls on that score: if he is paying attention, the boy has a chance at a kind of negative freedom, because he has not been trained since infancy to believe, as the girl has, that wedlock and the workaday are not just the norm, but as close to the ideal as can be expected. For as long as he could hold out, any boy in that room might still have a few years of relative freedom – so, of course, nobody stepped forward to claim Grace Noonan and, in spite of her public humiliation, or perhaps because of it, Grace stayed defiant to the end. She never did give up her secret – and quite a few of us admired her for that. Not just boys, but girls as well. We admired her for having seen the trap being laid for her and for how she refused to fall into it, or to push someone else in, as her mother had done before her.

Or that's what they thought, at least. On the other hand, I have no trouble believing the story I heard later, that when somebody asked Grace why she didn't tell, she said, 'Well, if I'd told them his name, we'd have had to get married and I didn't want to do that.'

'Why not?'

'Dunno, really,' Grace was reputed to have said. 'He just wasn't my type.'

And yet, for all I was supposed to know, for all I had seen and learned from the married people around me, it was luck and nothing else that kept me from falling into the exact same trap. Luck, in the form of Annette Winters's notion that there was such a thing as her type, and that I was not it. I might have been growing into a cliché boys' own world where the basic premises were

a) have sex with as many attractive girls as possible – by attractive, I mean not attractive to oneself, necessarily, but attractive in the eyes of others – and

b) keep moving so you don't get trapped

but I don't want to suggest that there was anything cold or cynical about all this. More of us actually liked the girls we knew than were prepared to admit it, but we only had to look around to *know* that, whatever we thought or felt when we were alone, romantic love – disco love – as constructed by the movies and TV and pop songs, was a carefully baited trap, intended to lock us for life into a routine of drudge labour and joyless domesticity, with nothing to take refuge in but alcohol and 'the football'. This wasn't about 'fear of commitment' (that cliché); it was about common sense. We had not forgotten that the word 'commitment' can be used in two, by no means contradictory, senses: i) being prepared to engage fully in a (disco) relationship, and ii) being contained in a psychiatric medical facility. We had to cram what living we wanted into a few good years, because work was a life sentence and marriage was a lifelong battle with someone terminally conditioned for nest building and social propriety – and the biggest irony of all was that the pleasure part, the sex part, the exquisite play that got you into all that hassle in the first place started to evaporate the moment you carried your bride over the threshold.

So, when people wonder why boys want to stay boys and never grow up, as if there really were some difficulty to that particular question, I find it embarrassing, because the answer is obvious. A boy gets to play; a man doesn't, or not officially anyway (forget all that squash ladder/Sunday league/pub cricket stuff; that's not play, it's competition. Try asking your opposite number in Finance if he wants to go out and toss a Frisbee around the park some lunchtime and see what happens). A man is obliged to act out the part scripted for him, all the while pretending that there's something genuinely fulfilling in being promoted to Deputy Sales Manager or being chosen as Employee of the Month by other men who, while not visibly smarter or more able than him, get paid a whole lot more. Men are police officers, husbands, company directors; men work in middle management and fret about sex and their position on that supposedly recreational squash ladder. Men lay down the law and take up arms. Men, to the boy I was, were dull, neuter, slightly stale when you got up close and infinitely tedious. The burdens they carried with such absurd solemnity seemed to me entirely fictitious and the presumption of authority that defined them to a standstill was utterly alien to how I imagined a just world to be, alien and pointless, and painstakingly justified, for each individual man, by a self-perpetuating system of titles and obligations that were unfailingly referred to as 'the real world'. To belong to that world was the prerequisite for success, and not to succeed on that world's terms was to fail.

So there we were: trapped. Boys in striped shirts and basketball shoes listening to Quicksilver Messenger Service and the Doors in our bedrooms, knowing it couldn't last. Boys smoking dope on the patch of waste ground behind the garages; boys fiddling with hooks and zips in front rooms and parked cars; boys going out alone in the cool of a summer's dawn to swim on that stretch of river only they know. Men in waiting, all, tagged with the sorrow of knowing pretty well what is to come and not wanting any part of it. Manhood is what the boy wants to avoid, as he grows into the mould, but he doesn't know how, other than by continuing to be a boy. Moving on, every time love turns from serious to solemn. Deferring that dread moment when it comes time to settle down and open a savings account, putting a little by every year till he's got enough to make the down payment on a house that looks just like every other jerry-built house on the estate. Laughing at the disco love lyrics on the radio and *Top of the Pops*. What would real success look like, for a boy who chose not to be that kind of a man, but grew at his own pace into the creature he could have been, had his future not been decided for him years ago? The boy's only answer is a desperate one, a beginner's guide to clutching at straws, but it's all he has and what it mostly consists of is refusal. Pyrrhic and half imagined as it is, his only victory is to let go and move on, for as long as he can, as decently as he can, for the thrill of that first meeting and the dark pleasure of the goodbye that keeps the heart in play, no gods above, no larks, no love song finer, only the drama that staying cannot confer, the exquisite and inevitable affirmation of every time we say goodbye.

All this might be a little crude, but I don't think it misrepresents the way my generation and class of boys thought and behaved, except in one key detail: that is, the question of 'whatever we thought or felt when we were alone'. I'm not saying it's true of everyone, but I know that, in my case, the drive to have sex and move on was based on a fear that, in all probability, quite a few of my classmates shared: the fear, not so much of The System as of my own profoundly romantic male nature. It took me a long time to work it out, and even longer to acknowledge it, but, looking back, I see that my teen self, contrary to appearances, had, in fact, been converted by my mother's radio into a hopeless romantic – and for all I know, if Annette Winters hadn't been so finicky about who might or might not have been her type, I could be married to her now, and wondering how in God's name I'd got myself tangled up in that particular mess. According to Oscar Wilde, 'marriage is the triumph of imagination over intelligence'; the trouble was, if you lived in a two-up two-down council house in Corby New Town, keeping a marriage alive took more imagination than most people could spare – and if any of us had been possessed of even the most basic intelligence, we would have seen right away that, in a society that worked so hard to keep us from loving, or even liking, ourselves, expecting us to love somebody else – not a type, but an actual person – was a bit much to ask.

THIRD DIGRESSION: ON NARCISSISM

There stands a fountain in a darksom wood,
Nor stain'd with falling leaves nor rising mud;
Untroubled by the breath of winds it rests,
Unsully'd by the touch of men or beasts;
High bow'rs of shady trees above it grow,
And rising grass and chearful greens below.
Pleas'd with the form and coolness of the place,
And over-heated by the morning chace,
Narcissus on the grassie verdure lyes:
But whilst within the chrystal fount he tries
To quench his heat, he feels new heats arise.
For as his own bright image he survey'd,
He fell in love with the fantastick shade;
And o'er the fair resemblance hung unmov'd,
Nor knew, fond youth! it was himself he lov'd.
The well-turn'd neck and shoulders he descries,
The spacious forehead, and the sparkling eyes;
The hands that Bacchus might not scorn to show,
And hair that round Apollo's head might flow;
With all the purple youthfulness of face,
That gently blushes in the wat'ry glass.

By his own flames consum'd the lover lyes,
And gives himself the wound by which he dies.
To the cold water oft he joins his lips,
Oft catching at the beauteous shade he dips
His arms, as often from himself he slips.
Nor knows he who it is his arms pursue
With eager clasps, but loves he knows not who.

What could, fond youth, this helpless passion move?
What kindled in thee this unpity'd love?
Thy own warm blush within the water glows,
With thee the colour'd shadow comes and goes,
Its empty being on thy self relies;
Step thou aside, and the frail charmer dies.[17]

Several interesting features in this account stand out, though perhaps the most important is the elusiveness of the shadow that 'comes and goes', and the fact that it is the lover who wounds himself, rather than being wounded by another. He creates the desire that overwhelms him: the Beloved's 'empty being' relies on his willingness to be charmed – but if he would only step aside, the 'frail charmer' would die away, leaving nothing behind but empty space.

In *Eros the Bittersweet*, Anne Carson explores the dynamics of this pursuit and evasion, (we note that Narcissus is out hunting when he finds the 'darksom' wood and its unsullied pool). The detail of her argument is too complex to go into

[17] From Book III of Ovid's *Metamorphoses*, tr. Joseph Addison, 1717.

here; simply expressed it revolves around the ancient paradox that if I want (i.e. lack) something, and if I succeed in taking possession of what I want, then I will, by definition, no longer want it. In short, the pleasure of romantic – or erotic – love is in the *wanting*, not the having, and any satisfaction leads quickly and inevitably to indifference. Thus, the only way to perpetuate such love is to be forever *on the point* of possession, simultaneously 'to possess and yet not to possess'. Assuming this argument holds (and for the romantic it seems to be the only escape from the terror that 'things will last'), Narcissus can be said to have found in his image the perfect Beloved, one he can neither possess nor lose; at the same time, because this image is actually himself, he knows that he will always retain his integrity, and not be overwhelmed by the neediness, or by the refusal, of the beloved other.

Yet another interesting detail of this myth – drawn from later, apocryphal material – is the suggestion that Narcissus was the original painter. The notion is discussed by Leon Battista Alberti in his *De Pictura*, where he claims that 'the true inventor of painting was Narcissus, that youth who, according to the poets, was transformed into a flower. And, since painting is the flower of all the arts, this story of Narcissus is most apt. For what is painting, if not an attempt, *through the discipline of art*, to embrace the surface of the pool in which we are reflected?' [My italics] Taking this notion, and the story of Narcissus as set out in Ovid, it is difficult not to think that Freud and his followers make a significant error in reducing the role of Narcissus to that of a mere emblem for infantile 'self-love', a developmental phase that, if it is not overcome on the road to normalised adult relations, will flower into a psychopathology. Indeed, this diagnosis not only seems an error but – given the significance of the Narcissus figure in the discipline of art – should also be seen as a missed opportunity.

So who is Narcissus, and what is his business here? An alternative to the commonly accepted reading might run as follows: When Narcissus sees the beautiful youth in the pool, he does not *know*, at first, that it is his reflection. (Ovid goes to some lengths to explain that, to begin with, he didn't know it was himself that he was seeing.) In that first glimpse, he loves what he sees; only *later* does he understand that what he loves is actually himself. He sees himself in the pool, along with all the other things (the sky, the trees, the world all about him), and he finds this vision beautiful – and *this* is the cause of his initial delight. Having believed himself to be alone, looking out at a world that was separate from him, he all of a sudden sees that he is *in* that world. He is as *real* and mysterious and beautiful as that world is – and yet he is also a separate, potentially knowable being. This is what he has been waiting for all along – and this is why he rejected Echo, because she did nothing but repeat back to him what he had only just that moment said (thus confirming him in his original solipsism). Echo was insufficient to his desires because she agreed with him all the time (one might argue that she would, by that token, be the ideal partner for a Freudian 'narcissist', i.e. for someone who is merely 'in love' with himself). Because Echo presented no challenge to him, he kept on waiting for something else, a true other to his other. He wanted to see himself as a knowable object in a given world, a separate creature, both in and of the world around him and, in rejecting Echo, he has rejected the world as mere reflection of his own wishes and needs (doing, in fact, the very opposite of what a Freudian narcissist would presumably do). Yet, when he falls in love with his own image – the image of himself in a world that is neither echo nor reflection – he is suddenly surrounded by the unexpected and the unpredictable. Now, everything is surprising and, now, of course, he is mortal. If he had not recognised himself in this world, he could have lived forever in his solipsistic state. That was what the gods had promised at his birth – and that, in a sense, is exactly what he does not want. What he *does* want is a world in which the discipline of real love is possible – real love, not the gratification offered by Echo's unquestioning regard – and the beginning of that discipline is to acknowledge the mystery of, and to choose to love, oneself. This will seem, no doubt, an idiosyncratic interpretation of the myth-story but I do not think it so very far-fetched and, represented in this way, the story of Narcissus can be seen, not as one of self-absorption and hunger for crude gratification, but as a parable of the first moment in which the emerging person knows him or herself as a singular, mysterious, attentive creature, in a world shared with others, ready to move beyond what Robert Graves has called 'the harsh pride of need' into the 'true power of singleness in love'.

In 1935, the year in which he died, Ian D. Suttie's one major publication, a critique of Freudian analysis entitled *The Origins of Love and Hate*, was published by Kegan Paul. It is a fascinating and, at times, inspiring book, one that is complex and far-reaching in its scrutiny of what he calls 'the taboo on tenderness'. Perhaps

Suttie's main difference with the Freudians arises over their seeming obsession with infant sexuality, almost to the exclusion of other concerns; against this he posits a notion of 'shared interest' which leads, not to neurotic and jealous possessiveness of the mother, but to an increased tenderness towards her and a growing sense of connection and attentiveness to their shared world, manifest, as the child grows, in a desire to make and share a culture and to enter into egalitarian love-friendships.

We have now to consider whether this attachment-to-mother is merely the sum of the infantile bodily needs and satisfactions which refer to her, or whether the *need for a mother is primarily presented to the child's mind as a need for company and as a discomfort in isolation.* I can see no way of settling this question conclusively, but the fact is indisputable that a need for company, moral encouragement, attention, protectiveness, leadership, etc., remains after all the sensory gratifications connected with the mother's body have become superfluous and have been surrendered. In my view this is a direct development of the primal attachment-to-mother, and, further, I think that play, cooperation, competition, and culture-interests generally are substitutes for the mutually caressing relationship of child and mother. *By these substitutes we put the whole social environment in the place once occupied by mother* – maintaining with it a mental or cultural rapport in lieu of the bodily relationship of caresses, etc., formerly enjoyed with the mother. A joint interest in *things* has replaced the reciprocal interest in *persons*; *friendship* has developed out of love.

True, the personal love and sympathy is preserved in friendship; but this differs from love in so far as it comes about by the *direction of attention upon the same things* (rather than upon each other), or by *the pursuit of the same activities even if these are not intrinsically useful* and gratifying, as is the case with much ritual, dance, etc. The interest is intensified even if it is not entirely created (artificial) by being *shared*; while the fact of sharing interest deepens the appreciation of the other person's presence even while it deprives it of sensual (or better of sensorial) qualities.[18]

This, then, is Suttie's view of the process of sublimation and it differs from the Freudians' analysis in two important ways: first, it dispenses with the need to 'define all pleasure or satisfaction as sexual', and, second, it brings to the fore the power of shared interest, leading to creative and appreciative play, and so to culture. In this analysis 'necessity [or need] is not the mother of invention; play is', and pathological attachment to the other, or the 'dread of loneliness' predicated on the unpredictability and wilfulness of that other, is transformed into a companionable state that allows for both the preservation of the self's, and respect for the other's, integrity. 'Originally,' Suttie says:

the Baby-Mother bond is vaguely and intuitively appreciated by the former as mutual absorption. By degrees the baby's expanding activities and sense-impressions change the character of this bond. A service rendered to the baby's

---

[18] Ian D. Suttie: *The Origins of Love and Hate* (all italics are Suttie's).

body and a caress are originally indistinguishable by it, but the baby's perceptions of and interest in its own body and its immediate surroundings grow rapidly under the influence of the mother's ministrations. In this way it develops Interest-in-Itself, the process Freud misconceives as Narcissism. It is of course arbitrary to say at what point the *companionship of love* becomes the *companionship of interest*, but there is no doubt that the feeling-relationship of the companions does change *as attention ceases to be absorbed wholly and reciprocally each in the other and becomes directed convergently to the same things.* Cooperative activities, identical or complementary attitudes to outside happenings, build up a world of *common meanings* which marks a differentiation from simple love wherein 'the world' of each is the other person. The simple direct bond has become a triangular relationship wherein external objects form the *medium of play.*[19]

This spirit of playfulness is what societal notions of love and romance set out to kill, transforming the lover into an infantile, possessive, highly neurotic sentimentalist. The playful, quite unsentimental, but deeply romantic Narcissus refuses the predictable responses Echo has to offer because he wants surprise, risk, a *world* – and that is precisely what a civilised society must refuse in order to achieve the discontented order that, for Freud, eventually became the last dark cul-de-sac of his philosophy. To call this spirit playful is not to diminish it

---

[19] Ibid. (all italics are Suttie's).

in any way: play is of the essence, play is, as Suttie says, the mother of invention. Play is how the universe gets to be itself – and because it calls for a full and alert engagement with the world, it requires élan, vim, *esprit*. At its heart, however, it calls into being and perpetuates the *erotic*. That is the true measure of the ability to be playful, and the one great taboo of the Authorised Version, dirt-poor, faux-Christian milieu where, according to my betters, I and all my kind were shaped in iniquity, and conceived in sin.[20] This is the great taboo – the taboo against erotic life, that is also, by extension, a taboo against the *thrawn*, the wild, the beglamoured, and, because a proper acknowledgement of mortality as a fact of life allows us to dwell fully in the now, it is intimately connected with the taboo against death. When that taboo is broken, even by the most innocent of sinners, an example has to be made, no matter how trivial the offence. Not everybody understands this but, when the need arises, everyone takes part in the ceremony as prescribed.

[20] Psalm 51:5

STRANGE DAYS

(*The Doors, 1967*)

It's not often that I remember the faces of men or boys. Every time I encounter a man I know (an acquaintance, even a friend), I am a little surprised: I recognise him, of course, but something is wrong, its as if one or other of the features (bright freckling across the nose, say, or dark brown hair, cut a little too short to disguise thinning), seems recently added, so the whole is transformed into something unfamiliar and I have to relearn it again, fitting the elements together like a PhotoFit through the first few moments of our conversation, during which time, I am sure, he knows that something is wrong and assumes that I am not in the least interested in what he is saying or, perhaps, that I have fallen prey to the sudden mistrust that, somewhere behind his assured, easy-going facade, he suspects is there in everyone he knows. Far too often, what we think about when we think about trust has something to do with speech, so I am stuck, just as often, with a lull in the conversation, a lull that doesn't quite develop into abandonment, a lull during which I seem to be lying, or think he is lying, or both. And sometimes, of course, I *am* lying. I can't help it. Sometimes I lie to fill the gaps; occasionally I lie because the truth is too dull to repeat yet again; fairly often, I lie because

I am stalling for time; more often still, I lie because I am afraid that this lull, this suspicious pause, will allow something to be seen that he or I would prefer to keep hidden.

Sometimes there are exceptions to this rule, but they are few and far between and there is no real logic to my remembering. For instance, I can close my eyes now and still picture the face of an old man I once met in a bar in northern California; he had very dark brown, almost black eyes and a half-smile that could switch from grim to wistful to celebratory in the wink of an eye; he told me that he had walked across America seven times and that he had once met Jack Kerouac and Neal Cassady in a pool hall in Denver. When I was nineteen, I encountered a man on the road near Thrapston; he was a couple of years older than me, with light brown hair and grey eyes, and though our encounter lasted for no more than a few minutes I remember him vividly because, during those few minutes, he died. I remember my Uncle John because his face was always the same, a set mask concealing a hard, wartime secret, and I remember John Mason because, by the time I met him, there was something in his features that I had never seen in anyone else. To most people, he was just the school retard by that time, but I saw something else in him, some vestige of a former self that I may well have imagined, having heard his story; though I like to think there is more to it than that. What I saw was barely a shadow, the merest hint of someone for whom life should have been a quest – and it was said that, before his accident, John Mason was quite a character. I didn't know him then, though. I met him several months after he fell from the railway bridge on Cottingham Road, and by then there was a gap in his eyes – not a hollowness, and not a vacancy, but a gap, a missing link in the fine detail of his gaze that made him seem, not so much far away as a little too close for comfort, his presence constantly blurring, as bodies do when they loom into another body's space. That accident of his had come of a dare: he'd been approaching the bridge with some friends when the others bet him that he couldn't walk across on the stone parapet while a train was passing underneath; naturally, he had taken the bet, because he was a spirited boy for whom everything seemed not just possible but easy. And, naturally, he fell.

His luck didn't run out entirely, however; for having fallen just as the train went clear of the bridge, he landed on empty tracks and the next train wouldn't come for some considerable time – so, if the other boys had stayed calm and weighed their options, they could have rescued him, or perhaps found someone nearby to help, but, being Corby boys and, so, guilty from birth, they ran away, scattering to their separate houses or to secret dens in the woods where they usually hid from consequences, and John Mason lay unconscious on the tracks for some time, before a man on his way to back shift at the Works came along and pulled him clear. By then, the damage was done and when John Mason woke in a hospital bed some time later, his parents barely knew him, for that accident had left him *thrawn*, a loose thread of wildness in the drab fabric of our humdrum town, where even the Living God we heard about in church was tame, unexceptional and, truth to tell, intolerably dull.

When he left the hospital, John Mason came back to school and it seems that, to begin with at least, his classmates were sympathetic, even considerate. However, it wasn't long before his condition posed a problem. Or rather, a series of problems that, with the onset of puberty, became impossible to ignore. I arrived at the same school a few months after his fall, determined to hate the place, unhappy, antisocial and angry at having been forced to move from Cowdenbeath – and the first person I encountered was this blurred, looming creature who, by now, had become foreign and difficult to everyone around him. I was fascinated. Not by his history, or by his actual condition, but by that hollow in his face and by the fact that he was, when I arrived, in the process of being quite deliberately *estranged* by his schoolmates. Not ostracised, but estranged; not persecuted or bullied, but set to one side and kept there by a surprisingly Byzantine system of looks and whispers, mocking smiles and sly shakings of the head, occasional, *sub rosa* threatening glances and half-gestures and, subtlest of all, but ever-present, the simple tyranny of the group. Many of that group had started out more or less well meaning, but their initial sympathy had been tested to its limit and now the majority had fallen into a pattern of ignoring him, while a few watched and waited for the least mistake or clumsy gesture, then jumped in to mock him back into silence and apathy. A few in the latter group – some of them his former friends – went so far as to say that it was wrong, keeping John Mason in a normal school, that he ought to be *put in an institution*, but from our very first encounter, when he loomed suddenly close and stared at me through that hollowed, shadowy face, before grinning stupidly as someone shifted him aside to interrogate the new boy, I chose to think of him as touched – by which I meant, without being able to put it into words, that some pagan god or earth angel had raked its jagged, loamy fingers through the jelly of his brain and left him marked forever, his face strangely unmasked, in spite of the shadows and gaps, the inner machinery of his soul nakedly visible there, if only one could learn how to read the signs.

Yet while most of his classmates were content to ignore John Mason, as long as he stayed out of the way and kept his mouth shut, there was one boy – to whom everyone referred, simply, as Foley – who couldn't draw the line at that. I have no clear memory of the boy's face, and if I recall his name now, it's only because he played a small part in John Mason's story. I remember his name, and I remember his presence in a purely abstract way: a mean, sloe-eyed whip of a boy already possessed to a remarkable degree by the ugly spirit, he was always accompanied by his best friend, Malky, a bulkier, sub-skinhead, but still unconvincing thug, with already noticeable signs of flabbiness to come in his neck and cheeks and something vaguely lilywhite about the eyes that probably made even his mother turn away from him in distaste. From the first, Foley seemed to take John Mason as a personal affront and, with occasional backup from Malky, it was his chief mission in life to keep him in line: if John spoke in class, Foley would heave a theatrical sigh and throw appealing looks at the teacher; if John started to help with the clearing up after art or woodwork, Foley would grab the broom or the jar of dirty paintbrushes before John could get to them and take them to the sink himself, scowling and muttering under his breath, while John stood staring in puzzlement for a long moment, before moving back into a safe corner. In the playground, Foley and Malky would team up to keep

John out of the game during football or rounders; if he jumped into the middle of an impromptu game of tag or British Bulldogs, they would chase after him, whooping and catcalling, till he gave up and ran back to from where he came; if he tried to get into a conversation, they would stop talking and stare at him blankly till he turned away, sometimes blinking back tears as the banter continued without him. He was a non-person, a foreign body in our midst and, to varying degrees, all the kids in that school collaborated in his estrangement.

This state of affairs continued for a couple of years and, while not everyone liked what was happening, nobody thought to speak out against it. As for me, I was as guilty, and possibly guiltier than the rest: as disgusted as I was by the likes of Foley and Malky, I did nothing and said nothing; I just watched the continuing story unfold, quietly hoping that John would one day snap and lash out, not just at his two main persecutors, but at the whole group. To the uprooted and angry child I was then, the entire school was hateful, and the sad, low-level drama I envisaged – something akin to an old-style Western, or a revenger's tragedy, where five acts are taken up with prevarication and second chances, before the hero finally, and very decisively, *does something* – was at least a distraction from an otherwise desperately boring regime of badly taught maths and the creation of hand-turned wooden ashtrays.

Real life isn't like the movies, though – as much of a cliché as that sounds now, I still recall the dismay I felt when I realised that Shane didn't actually exist and that Tybalt would have made mincemeat of a real, flesh-and-blood Romeo. In real life, the gentle giants fail to retaliate once too often and we give up on them in disgust; in real life, we start to despise ourselves for ever being so naive as to have hoped for justice and, in real life, the bad kids grow up and get a little wiser, and start playing another game – in the case of Foley and Malky, the game of pretending to befriend John Mason, all the better to scapegoat him. It was a good tactic: eager to show off to his new-found buddies, John was easily persuaded to get up halfway through class and deliver a hard, scabbed crab apple to Miss Gould, our more than usually miserable maths teacher, or to call out meaningless but strangely obscene-sounding responses during morning assembly. Soon, some little piece of farce was happening on a more or less weekly basis but, no matter what the offence, or who interrogated him, John would never reveal who had put him to it.

All this time, Malky and Foley studied him like a pair of ferrets, alert to every sign of a possible opening. Finally, it became clear that John was developing some very specific, but unarticulated feeling – a fondness? lust? the usual confused attraction of the young teenaged – for a petite, somewhat timorous girl called Angela Laverty and, apart from his erstwhile friends, everyone in the school, from pupils to teachers to dinner ladies to the janitor, fell under the spell of a fascinated apprehension. Something was going to happen, we all sensed it, but nothing could be done and there was still hope that it would manifest itself in some innocent, or only mildly embarrassing, way. Oddly enough, the only person in the entire school who seemed, or at least pretended to be, blissfully unaware of John Mason's regard for her was Angela – and for a long time, John kept himself at a reasonable distance, his eyes following the object of his affections wherever she went, a bemused smile playing about his lips, while Foley and Malky looked on, waiting for their moment to pounce. For a time, I thought they were taking too long; soon, the playground would empty for the summer and their chance would be gone. Still, they waited – and then, just when I was beginning to think they had grown tired of the sport, John chased Angela into the dankest corner of the playground, unzipped his flies and said something nobody who was close to the action could repeat precisely later, though a couple of them said they were prepared to swear on the Holy Bible that it had to do with sucking. What was most impressive, however, what resonated across the playground and down the corridors into the staffroom, was the sound of Angela's screams. Whatever actual words John had used, everybody knew that those terms weren't any part of his vocabulary, but it was Angela's voice that determined the outcome. It may be that she'd been holding back that scream for years, it may be that her horror originated in something else entirely, but it was John Mason's satyr-like advances that allowed them to emerge from the well of her body and that was the deciding factor in the investigation that ensued. When that investigation ended, John Mason disappeared from our lives and Foley and Malky went around smirking for weeks.

Where John Mason's disappearance had taken him was the topic of whispered conversation for a while – he's in a madhouse, he's been scheduled for a lobotomy – but not for as long as I would have expected. The truth was, most people were glad to forget him. The official line was that, after 'the incident' in the playground – for which John was held blameless, because he didn't really understand what he was doing – he was now attending a very special school where they had 'the facilities to give him the dedicated support and attention he required'. Of course, it didn't take much imagination to see through this, though I wasn't at all sure what I thought his real circumstances were. I did spend a rainy Saturday afternoon at the town library, going through the one book they had about the treatment of mental illness and, based on what were probably a slew of false assumptions, I pictured John growing old in some drab institution, a big-boned, clumsy masquerade of a man, propped in a grubby armchair in tartan slippers and a pair of striped pyjamas, staring into space and frightened of every loud word or passing shadow. On the other hand, it was more likely that he would just be bored, hideously bored and as bewildered by his captivity as a zoo animal. For a while, he may well have resisted, maybe he even fought until they gave him the necessary medication, but the necessary medication, no matter how hard you fight it, is always perversely sweet when it comes and, like Ulysses' shipmates in 'hollow Lotos-land', I imagine him slipping out of boredom into that stupor where 'all things have rest, and ripen toward the grave / In silence – ripen, fall, and cease' – and when cessation came, I like to suppose that it entered quietly, like a kindly assassin, delivering the final mercy on some damp August afternoon with a cup of sweet, milky tea, and a plate of digestive biscuits and closing the book on whatever it was I had seen in John Mason's face, all those years before.

FOURTH DIGRESSION: ON LOST GIRL SYNDROME

> She lived unknown, and few could know
> When Lucy ceased to be;
> But she is in her grave, and, oh,
> The difference to me.
>
> [William Wordsworth]

In Rian Johnson's 2005 high-school-movie-meets-film-noir debut, *Brick*, a hard-bitten, highly intelligent and perversely stubborn boy named Brendan finds his former girlfriend in a storm drain, apparently the victim of a murder. The girl is still recognisably beautiful, but already slipping towards the formlessness of death: soon, all the colour will drain away, even the dirty gold of her hair and the sad gaudy of her almost fluorescently bright plastic bangles. As the plot unfolds, we learn that, although she was discovered in water, one arm reaching out or up, as if trying to regain the surface, her body heavy with the weight of the flood, this girl did not die of drowning. Nevertheless, the initial image is so strong that it is immediately reminiscent of any number of Victorian paintings where a girl – a fallen woman, Ophelia, some fair maiden from Arthurian legend – is shown immersed, or drowned, in a lake or river. In G. F. Watts's rather touching morality painting, *Found Drowned*, for example, a prostitute, apparently hauled from the Thames in the early hours of the morning, is laid out like some dead saint in a crypt. Behind her, the sky is still dark – only the morning star on the horizon – yet she herself is oddly lit, her reddish and brown clothes almost luminescent, though her face is cold and ashen. Publicly, at least, Watts's purpose in making this painting was commonplace moral didacticism: his drowned girl is real, the victim of a society that allowed young women to slide into poverty and forced prostitution in Victorian London's slums.

Yet it is also true that, like the girl in the storm drain, or Ophelia in her shroud of waterweed, she stands for a different type of killing, for an unseen, but equally mysterious death in the alembic of Brendan's psyche. Not the death of a girl at all, but the abandonment of that intelligent, stubborn boy's full potential, as he reluctantly stumbles forward into the bluff and bluster of workaday manhood. In allegorical terms, that soul-self is most often seen as a girl, because a seeming girlishness is what the boy appears to give up in order to *be a man*, but this substitution serves two purposes: first, the death of the girl gives the boy something to mourn, in the realm of myth; second, it gives him a vehicle to conceal his deepest nature, a story in which to freeze her forever, in the eternity of the possible. The lost self as drowned girl becomes at once eternally beautiful, because she is not carried forward into the sheer tedium of grown manhood and, at the same time, she is made other, estranged, and so more capable of being discarded. This is the work that the drowned girl does in male art: she remains present as an image and, at the same time, forever untouchable, at once intimate and impossibly distant, like the star of the morning, or the dark continuum of the erotic current wherein she is concealed.

Found drowned

The drowned girl, the lost girl of boyhood, is everywhere in men's stories. She appears in poetry and paintings, films and novels, dance routines and erotica, but she is never quite what she seems and her presence is almost entirely abstract, a life that ends before it has the opportunity even to draw breath, a ghost who is both discarded Narcissus and possible lover and so must immediately be locked into a lifelong sleep before she has time to waken and look around. Accounts of the Trojan War tell us that Agamemnon achieves full kingship when he offers his daughter, Iphigenia, for sacrifice – to be a leader of men, he has to surrender his 'feminine side' – but surely this notion of a man's feminine side is as crude as all the other weak notions about 'gender' that we cobble together in the brute process of socialisation. But what if it is something else he loses, something for which the girl figure stands in only a loose, essentially allegorical, way? We cannot help but feel that Agamemnon is not just surrendering his 'feminine side' in this sacrifice: he is giving up the fullness of his soul, the pleroma, and this can no more be 'gendered' than beauty, or grace.[21]

---

[21] Contrast the story of Arjuna, who enters into the final stage of warrior-hood only after serving a year's term, in disguise, as a dancing teacher, a role

What if it is too easy to see the allegory of the drowned or lost or sacrificed girl as yet another example of (an assuredly all-too-common) misogyny? Certainly, misogyny doesn't explain the plainly elegiac quality of the images. In many cases, the girl is portrayed as a beloved corpse, some lost beauty with a life and ways of her own, unfairly stolen away by fate or, like Iphigenia, by the demands of public life. Moreover, in all these stories, there is one significant difference between the dead girl and the raped, murdered and mutilated women so familiar from mainstream cinema and the evening news. For what is significant about our lost girls, from Wordsworth's Lucy Gray (whose disappearance into a snowy landscape is recorded in a poem whose full title is 'Lucy Gray, or Solitude') to Otto Preminger's Laura (seen only as a beautiful, highly stylised portrait for the first part of the movie), is that she is not really dead at all. She is somewhere else, a part of 'nature', a star, a spirit, a motion. Even the Virgin Mary, the great Western archetype of the lost girl, is not permitted to die, but is 'assumed' into Heaven, suspended, yet still present, and so preserved as an eternal possibility – though she is not allowed to continue as a living creature.

A slumber did my spirit seal

You either feel it, or you don't: boys are obliged to discard something in their late teens, in the process of becoming *grown*

---

normally considered effete. The warrior achieves fullness, not by expunging one aspect of his being, but by learning how to use everything and anything that comes to hand.

men. It's not entirely gone, not altogether lost, perhaps, but it cannot be grasped, or properly named. We are obliged to speak about it in allegory and often the story is that of a girl, or a girl-like creature, who, whether drowned, sacrificed or buried alive, must be hidden away in the dark where *nobody* can find her. As a grown man, you either feel it or you don't – and if you don't, the lack is still visible to those around you. If you do feel it, you mourn, and the grief can manifest itself in dramatic forms. Alcohol, drugs, obsession, self-harm, random addiction to obscure and unglamorous dangers. Yet it is still better to feel it than not. Not to feel it means to die without ever being haunted – and who would wish for that? Besides, loss is always accompanied by a possible discovery, or a possible transformation, and if a man only has the imaginative ability needed to perform a resurrection, the hidden girl can return in a different form, to participate in the story at last, or she can be transformed into something other, some fantastical, even freakish creature, recovered from the dark reaches of sleep.

Iphigenia in Tauris

According to some legends, Iphigenia is not actually killed. Instead, Artemis – like God in the story of Isaac – substitutes a goat (a form of the god Pan) for the doomed girl, then carries her away to Tauris, where she became a priestess. In other words, though Agamemnon gives her up for sacrifice, she does not die, but remains hidden from the world, until the time comes to play her part in the next stage of the myth, saving her brother from certain death at the hands of the Tauri, then assisting in his reconciliation with the Erinyes, so that he may return to assume his rightful position among the Mycenaeans. In this story, the necessary reversal is achieved: one man wins a highly prized, but compromised, kingship by allowing the ur-girl to be sacrificed, but his son grows into full manhood – and is freed from his former guilt – only when he offers himself as a sacrifice to the very girl his father had sacrificed. Overall, this myth tells us of the right way of kingship, to be sure, but it also reminds us that the lost girl never dies, she simply bides her time, rolled around in earth's diurnal course, till the moment of re-emergence.

Memories of an imaginary festival

I am in the bar of a typical corporate hotel in a foreign city; it doesn't matter which. I order a vodka tonic and the barman, a sad-faced, jowly being with baggy eyes and a lonely, blood-hound stare, brings it to me with a bone-white, angular, faintly Scandinavian-style bowl piled high with salted almonds. There's nobody else here, just me and this man who, having served my drink, retreats back into the little pool of distance that any good barman can find when he needs it. There's a statement going on here that I know and rather enjoy: what he is saying is that, no matter how many or how few customers he has, no matter how many conversations he gets into, he is still alone, still on the other side of that counter – and he likes it that way. If he's ever lonely, it's only for a drink or a woman; company is something he can live without.

I take a first sip of vodka. This is the best time, when the evening is just beginning and anything is possible, but also because anticipation is better than most of the outcomes that actually happen. I scoop a handful of almonds from the Swedish-style bowl and eat them one by one. They are wonderful. I didn't even know I liked salted almonds, but I can't stop eating them, scooping them out and eating steadily for the sweet, almost milky flavour, and soon the bowl is empty – and as I eat, it comes to me that, at moments like this, yes, but also in some far place at the back of my head, I am, in some modest and ineffable way, supremely happy. Or perhaps not happy so much as given to fleeting moments of good fortune, the god-in-the-details sense of being obliged and permitted to inhabit a persistently surprising and mysterious world.

I am so caught up in these simple pleasures that I have yet to notice the young man who has come into the bar and settled on to the stool next to mine – though when I look up and finally take notice, I see that he has been watching me, waiting to start up a conversation, as is the custom in hotels like this one, and in situations like ours. The young man's name is Simon; he is not in the city on business, but lives here and is inexplicably keen to give the impression that he knows his way about the place. The club scene. The burgeoning indie-music scene. Other *scenes* that are only implied. After a few drinks, he invites me to a party on the north side of town, a party in a warehouse building with live music and an arty crowd and everything that goes with that and, though I have the feeling I am going to regret it, I end up following him into the night, in search of some phantom that neither of us really believes in. On the way, we drop by his house for what he calls *reinforcements* – and I immediately want to stop the carousel and get off, I'm so taken with his clean, well-lighted kitchen, all pine

wood and stone and tall jars of preserves on the shelves, like
the kitchen a drowned girl might have made, given the chance.
As we sit there, in a wreath of greeny smoke, I can't stop talking
about how much I like it, going so far beyond the usual *politesse*
that it starts to feel uncomfortable for us both – yet even as I
recognise this, I can't stop. Simon could easily put this enthu-
siasm for the decor down to childish irony, or my creeping
inebriation, but he goes to what soon feels like unnecessary
lengths to point out that it's not really his kitchen anyway, that
it just goes with the rented apartment, before he suddenly jumps
up and says that it's time to move on, that he has to make
contact with the girl who is organising the night, to find out
where exactly the party is going to be. He can see that I am
reluctant to leave, and this makes him anxious, but after a while
we catch another taxi to a kind of warehouse district and go
wandering about the side streets, music somewhere amid the
brickwork, a clear white moon high above us, silvery lights
everywhere, other people passing by, occasionally stopping to
talk or smoke, but no girl, or not to begin with. After a short
while, I'm regretting this wild goose chase, just as I thought I
would, and I'm aware that I really have no idea where I am,
but I'm also watching Simon, who seems more and more like
a man who is trying to find his way back, from somewhere I
recognise, to a place I can scarcely even begin to picture. I'm
not sure he can picture it either, but it isn't here, where we are
waiting, not even when the girl finally shows, a *Brick* kind of
girl, to be sure, but still only a girl. But then, it's not about the
girl, it's about the waiting, and the darkness over our heads
and, more than anything else, it's about that promise of a return,

about who we might arrive at when we come to the magical place we would know at a glance as soon as we stopped being the grown men we never intended to become.

Those eyes, how familiar they seem

In Georges Franju's film *Les yeux sans visage*, the lost girl is not dead, but hidden away, hopelessly disfigured after an accident for which her father was responsible. In fact, the girls who die in the film are not this ur-girl, but young women encountered at random and brought to a dark house beyond the suburbs, where their faces are surgically removed, in order to provide transplants for the faceless daughter. Nevertheless, *Les yeux sans visage* fits the drowned-girl pattern: the lost girl is as close as it is possible to be to a spirit, a slender ghost in a sterilised mask, looking out at a world in which she cannot participate, while those around her – the father, his beautiful and terrifying assistant, the police – pursue their various agendas. This girl has no agenda; she has no social presence, no face. Yet she is the truth of the film and her loss, though inevitable, is both tragic and strangely celebratory. What it celebrates is, perhaps, open to dispute, though it is hard not to imagine that somewhere, buried deep in this modern myth, is a sense that the lost girl is some damaged fragment of the boy, hopelessly disfigured by the process of socialisation and kept secret in a dark hinterland, lacking a face or a meaningful role in the outer world, yet still present, or almost so: a ghost waiting to be found and resurrected, or a trick of the light, in the hazy reaches of no-man's-land.

That laugh, that floats on the summer night

The grown man has still to be determined. He knows the feeling of *something half remembered,* of *something that never happened.* He knows the feeling of recognising *someone that he's never met as far as he can tell.* What attracts him? The one thing he lacks.

That was Laura, but she's only a dream

Nevertheless, if this allegory is tragic for those who *do* believe – if it indicates a reason for mourning – it also reminds us that the drowned girl is never wholly lost. She is there, in the morning star, in water, in the dark house, with rocks, and stones, and trees. She is not dead, only set aside. Set aside from the darkening gaze of public existence. Set aside for the night, for solitude. Given the right circumstances, she might even return, not as some chaste daughter of Artemis, but as a gorgeous and beglamoured freak, something more creaturely than anyone thought possible, a child of Pan, a strand of the true Dionysian Mystery.

Queen Jane, Approximately

There is no greater disaster in the spiritual life than to be immersed in unreality, for life is maintained and nourished in us by our vital relation with realities outside and above us. When our life feeds on unreality, it must starve. It must therefore die. There is no greater misery than to mistake this fruitless death for the true, fruitful and sacrificial 'death' by which we enter into life.[22]

---

[22] Thomas Merton: *Thoughts in Solitude.*

Solitude is appealing, because it is only when we are alone that we find the trail of footprints leading away into the snow that might bring us to Lucy, or allow us a glimpse of the eyes without a face staring back at us from the dark windows of houses that seem so ordinary by day. Still, *the world must be peopled* – and the best purpose of turning to solitude is to enrich the communal life. As Merton also says: *And your solitude will bear immense fruit in the souls of men you will never see on earth.*

Yet even as we see that we *must* live with others, in public, we also have to live with the creatures we might have become and sometimes the conflict is close to overwhelming, especially when it is difficult to distinguish one from the other, to separate the inward spirits from the bodies moving around us: as bright as they are and as innocent as they seem of this day's fear or recompense, the mutilated and disfigured ghosts we hide away in the dark can take apparently solid form, for hours or days at a time, when we imagine ourselves partners in some external drama of love or anger or deep hatred. Or they can flicker to the surface momentarily in an unguarded moment, as when a man in late-middle age, so far from his lost soul now that it really can be treated as a mere legend, licks his finger to turn the pages of the book he is reading and is immediately trans-formed into something other, a soul part-girl, part-animal, betrayed in this gesture he learned unconsciously half a century ago, as he watched his mother turn the pages of a family Bible, or sat staring into the fire, licking the tips of his fingers in an unconscious imitation of the family cat, curled up in the chair opposite, fastidiously licking her paws and washing the deep rich coat of fur and musk that, for years, he has secretly coveted.

Memories of an imaginary festival

It takes some time to get back from the warehouse-district party
to the place where I am supposed to be and, by the time I do,
I have forgotten why I came to this city in the first place. Simon
has disappeared, and I have vague memories of some indiscre-
tion on his part, something I cannot recall but *feel* as either
pathetic or shameful. I have no duties here that I can remember,
but I know it is not time yet for me to depart, so I sit in the
hotel bar for the next three days, watching the ice-hockey play-
offs and talking to grown men about the things grown men in
bars talk about. Sports, to begin with, or music, but later, when
alcohol has eroded our defensive lines, aimless and occasionally
moving tales of what a pyrrhic victory it is to be a grown man,
stories that barely contain an undercurrent of rebellion,
suggesting – an idea so utterly logical as to defy utterance – that
there is no better indication of sanity than the midlife crisis.
Outside, the weather has changed; it is cold, overcast, with
occasional sleety showers. Inside, around the bar, we tell stories
that skirt around, or mock, or make banal or ironic movies out
of what we know we have lost, even though we have no way
of properly naming it. We all have the air of men who want
to go back to something; only we don't know what it is. We're
not fools and I think we all know that this isn't real mourning
– because mourning, when conducted well, is a healing process,
while we are simply wallowing in our grief – but what we have
forgotten is the fact that, even if the grown man cannot go
back and restore the drowned girl to the light, he can still go
forward to find the magical animal into which she has been
transformed – and where she is waiting, as Plato's divided souls

wait, to restore and to be restored. In some Inuit carvings this transformation is captured in obsidian or bone – and the striking fact about these works is the surprise on each man's face, as if he doesn't quite believe that what he hoped for is actually happening. What these works also tell us, however, is that, no matter what happens in the dark realm of the public, the possibility remains that it is not inevitable that everyone born male will become a mere man. Arjuna becomes a dancing teacher and so finds the last virtue he needs to become the greatest of all warriors, Orestes finds the girl-soul his father relinquished and is rescued from madness and the persecution of the Erinyes; for the rest of us, the drowned girl remains, in the depths of the water, or hidden in the darkness of our own houses, a ghostly stranger self among all the other stranger selves and possible variants of being that we conceal.

FEAST OF THE MAU MAU / PORTRAIT
OF HEZEKIAH TRAMBLES

(Screamin' Jay Hawkins, 1969 / Diane Arbus, 1960)

He's Screamin' Jay Hawkins and he's a wild man, so bug off.[23]

Screamin' Jay Hawkins wasn't always a wild man. He had originally conceived 'I Put a Spell on You' as a blues ballad, a sophisticated love song, possibly in a similar mould to Nina Simone's cover (like Simone, he had trained as a classical pianist, back in his Cleveland days). When he got to the studio to record the song, however, the producer 'got everybody drunk, and we came out with this weird version . . . Before, I was just a normal blues singer. I was just Jay Hawkins. It all sort of fell into place. I found out I could do more destroying a song and screaming it to death.' Once again, we shouldn't accept everything Hawkins says as gospel, but it seems that shock-rock was born during that drunken night in the studio (a night Hawkins

---

[23] A line from the Jim Jarmusch film, *Stranger than Paradise*, made in 1984. The line is delivered by Eszter Balint, also a musician, whose best-known album is entitled *Mud*.

claimed not to remember afterwards), and it took off after DJ Alan Freed offered the singer $300 (real money in 1957) to emerge from a coffin onstage, dressed in a black cape. When Hawkins then added voodoo charms, nose bones and Henry the smoking skull to the routine, he was transformed into 'the black Vincent Price' – but he was also painted into a novelty act corner that he never quite escaped. Just as Louis Armstrong was accused of being an Uncle Tom for mugging and rolling his eyes for the white folks on the Bing Crosby show,[24] just as Hendrix seemed to trivialise his gift by playing guitar with his teeth (a trick he picked up from Butch Snipes, or perhaps from Buddy Guy), Screamin' Jay belonged to a long line of black entertainers whose genius was obscured, or at best compromised, by what some people saw as 'vulgar' showmanship and eccentricity. Yet his was genius in its baroque form; a gift that, like soul or *glamourie*, is not a possession or a character attribute, but a visitation, a grace event in which the subject becomes the teller of the aboriginal narrative. This grace event can lead to moments of extraordinary and recognisable beauty, but it can also lead to madness, possession, terror. To the dark end of the fair – or to the freak show. Back then, and maybe still, the people who ran the mainstream – the record companies, the DJs, the TV producers – didn't recognise that kind of genius and when it turned up they didn't know what to do other than poke at it with a stick and play for laughs. No better way to

---

[24] 'I never tried to prove nothing,' Armstrong said, 'just always wanted to give a good show. My life has been my music, it's always come first. But the music ain't worth nothing if you can't lay it on the public. The main thing is to live for that audience 'cause what you're there for is to please the people.'

protect Joe Public from the *real,* cask-strength, blackwater culvert of mojo-infested, King Snake crawling, canned heat and swamp tainted devil's music than to dress it up in a vampire costume, stick a bone through its nose and shove it onstage at Halloween for everyone to laugh at. When it gets to that point, all the baroque genius has left is irony and conscious self-parody,[25] but most of the time, the audience of frat boys and feathers-and-cream American girls doesn't even get that.

Freaks was a thing I photographed a lot. It was one of the first things I photographed and it had a terrific kind of excitement for me. I just used to adore them. I still do adore some of them. I don't quite mean they're my best friends but they made me feel a mixture of shame and awe. There's a quality of legend about freaks. Like a person in a fairy tale who stops you and demands that you answer a riddle. Most people go through life dreading they'll have a traumatic experience. Freaks were born with their trauma. They've already passed their test in life. They're aristocrats.

Diane Arbus

One of the freaks Diane Arbus photographed was Hezekiah Trambles (aka Congo, the Jungle Creep), who performed

[25] A wonderful example can be seen on *The Merv Griffin Show* (1966), where Hawkins displays his comic gifts to the full, after being introduced as a 'young man' with 'a great blues style, plus one of the wildest singing gimmicks I have ever heard, and it may not scare you but I guarantee you, when he's performing, you won't be going to the refrigerator'.

five times a day at Hubert's Dime Museum, on 42nd and Broadway, Times Square. The picture she took of him in 1960, made famous later when it appeared on the cover of the Rolling Stones album *Exile on Main Street*, shows a dishevelled man with thick, unruly hair, who, surprisingly perhaps, seems more fearful than frightening.[26] Trambles, whom Arbus described as 'terrible as anything', wore a glorious fright wig, black tights and animal skins, and, like Screamin' Jay, had a fondness for 'savage' totem objects and talismans. He played right into the crowd's prejudices, shambling about muttering incomprehensibly in his own variant of darkest African Ooga-Booga, while swallowing lit cigarettes and performing other dubious 'magic' acts; in real life, he wasn't from the Congo; he was a gay Haitian man who liked to dress up and promenade around Times Square. In most senses of the word, Trambles wasn't a freak at all, but he was definitely a member of Arbus's aristocracy. Arbus had been insulated as a child, kept away from anyone and any situation that might upset her, which apparently included everything from the genuinely disturbing facts of life to the ordinary poor. No surprise, then, that she grew up wanting to taste the reality from which she had been shielded. What is surprising, however, is that she felt so at home at the dark end of the fair. 'Nothing is ever the same as they said it was,' she said. 'It's what I've never seen before that I recognise.' She may have romanticised the 'aristocrats' she met there, but it would be wrong to suggest, as Susan Sontag does in her astonishing attack[27] on Arbus's

---

[26] This is the 'postcard' directly beneath the word 'Exile'.

[27] 'Most of Arbus's work lies within the Warhol aesthetic, that is, defines itself

work (in *On Photography*, 1977, arguably the most disingenuous book on that art ever published), that her 'freak' pictures are merely 'quaint'.[28] Not surprisingly, Arbus saw the world in quite another light, even as a child: 'There are and have been and will be an infinite number of things on earth,' she wrote in a

---

in relation to the twin poles of boringness and freakishness; but it doesn't have the Warhol style. Arbus had neither Warhol's narcissism and genius for publicity nor the self-protective blandness with which he insulates himself from the freaky, nor his sentimentality. It is unlikely that Warhol, who comes from a working-class family, ever felt any ambivalence toward success which afflicted the children of the Jewish upper middle classes in the 1960s. To someone raised as a Catholic, like Warhol (and virtually everyone in his gang), a fascination with evil comes much more genuinely than it does to someone from a Jewish background. Compared with Warhol, Arbus seems strikingly vulnerable, innocent – and certainly more pessimistic. Her Dantesque vision of the city (and the suburbs) has no reserves of irony. Although much of Arbus's material is the same as that depicted in, say, Warhol's *Chelsea Girls* (1966) . . . for Arbus, both freaks and Middle America were equally exotic: a boy marching in a pro-war parade and a Levittown housewife were as alien as a dwarf or a transvestite; lower-middle-class suburbia was as remote as Times Square, lunatic asylums, and gay bars. Arbus's work expressed her turn against what was public (as she experienced it), conventional, safe, reassuring – and boring – in favor of what was private, hidden, ugly, dangerous, and fascinating. These contrasts, now, seem almost quaint. What is safe no longer monopolizes public imagery. The freakish is no longer a private zone, difficult of access. People who are bizarre, in sexual disgrace, emotionally vacant are seen daily on the newsstands, on TV, in the subways. Hobbesian man roams the streets, quite visible, with glitter in his hair.'

[28] The trouble with Sontag is that, at some level, she thought art should be good for you; there is an underlying desire for a kind of old-world, humanist wholesomeness.

school essay in 1939. 'Individuals all different, all wanting different things, all knowing different things, all loving different things, all looking different. Everything that has ever been on earth has been different from every other thing. That is what I love: the differentness, the uniqueness of all things and the importance of life . . . I see the divineness in ordinary things.'

JUST MY IMAGINATION (RUNNING AWAY WITH ME)

(*The Temptations, 1971*)

I started taking photographs when I was sixteen, just a few weeks after I was first introduced to LSD. My first camera was a 1950s Ensign Ranger, which I bought in a tatty bric-a-brac shop in Kettering. I had just been expelled from school and, having tried and failed to get a job as a clerical assistant in a local import–export business, I let my mother persuade me to continue my education at Kettering Technical College, signing up for A-level courses in French, Spanish, English and – I have no idea what possessed me here – Sociology. My mother wanted me go to university, partly because my cousin John, having graduated *magna cum laude* from Edinburgh, had just got a fancy research job working for Kodak, but she also thought that I would never make anything of my life if I didn't get a degree and become *a professional person*. I wanted my mother to be happy and, considering I had nothing better to do, I walked down to the end of the street every morning and hopped on a bus that meandered through fields of grain and picturesque Northamptonshire villages for seven miles, before dropping me off just opposite Kettering library, an old red-brick building

next to the Alfred East Gallery with a rather grand feel to it
(or grand, at least, to a boy from Corby New Town). Alfred
East was a semi-famous painter, best known for his scenes of
Oriental life: women in silk kimonos, temple gardens, brightly
coloured street markets reminiscent of Japanese woodblock
prints, only softer, as if Hokusai had suddenly fallen under the
spell of the Barbizon School. I didn't know much about art
but, fairly soon, I was spending most of my time there, or in
the little museum at the foot of the town, where they had big
cabinets full of birds' eggs and brightly coloured beetles.
Sociology was even duller than I had expected, my French and
Spanish classes were run by a woman whom I found so attractive
I could hardly bear to be in the same room as her, and
the English teacher was a prim old harridan who seemed to
hate every other member of her sex. (Her finest moment came
on the afternoon she arrived late to class, and finding a pretty
student called Susannah brushing her hair, slapped the girl's
hand and told her not to do that in front of the boys, because
it might *inflame* them.)

It was the Alfred East Gallery that inflamed me, however; not
because the pictures were important or valuable, but because it
was obvious to me from the first that Alfred East was after something that I knew about, but couldn't put a name to. Something
I lacked. Something *sumptuous*. Not rare, and not rich in the way
I understood rich at that time: on the contrary, his subject matter
was commonplace, and nothing about it looked extravagant. He
painted French landscapes and English lakes, and they were not
dissimilar to the places I had visited on family holidays, or even
from the farmland through which I travelled in the bus to college,

but even the Japanese scenes didn't seem particularly exotic. What was *rich* about these paintings was the colour. It was as if someone had reached up and found the switch that turned the lights on in my everyday world – everything was deeper, stronger, more erotic. In an Alfred East painting, things looked the way they looked on LSD. Not so much strange as new. Not dreamlike and not at all unreal. Things were as they were, only more so, like the objects and animals in an illuminated manuscript.

My first tab was a pink microdot, given to me free by a lank-haired boy I met on the bus a week after I started college. For some time, I'd been smoking hash and downing the odd handful of bennies or barbs whenever I could get them, but I wasn't in the least prepared for what LSD would do to my world. The boy – whose name was Pat – advised me to keep the tab till I was in a place where I felt comfortable and safe, but I thought he was just being dramatic, so I dropped it a few minutes after we parted, on the short walk to college. A half-hour later, I was beginning to think I'd been taken for a ride and was heading off to my first class of the day when the world suddenly lit up like a Christmas tree. Well, that's not it exactly, but there *was* a new sense of things being lit from within, and there was so much detail to my surroundings that I felt I was in danger of being overwhelmed by it all – and then I *was* overwhelmed. Everything – colour, sound, form, light – was more vivid than it had ever seemed before, yet I didn't think of this vividness as an illusion brought about by the drug. On the contrary, I knew, without a doubt, that this was how things really were, and that I had simply lost, or perhaps never gained, the ability to *see*.

There is no point in trying to describe an acid trip. Even if it were possible to do so, it would take far too long: LSD robs the mind of its learned sense of clock time and, because all the usual boundaries and conventions dissolve within the first fifteen minutes of the trip, it makes a mockery of what my sociology teachers fondly referred to as 'objectivity'. There *is* no clock time on acid; there *is* no objectivity. Instead, everything becomes qualitative. Everything is glamoured, in the old and full sense. What I can say is that I skipped classes that day and went, first to the Alfred East Gallery and then, when I became aware of the fact that other people were overtly aware of me, to the park by the museum, where I sat and gazed at a hedge, watching the leaves turn in the light wind that gusted through the gardens, and through my mind, all that afternoon. By the time I came down enough to think about going home, it was evening. I was still tripping, but I didn't think it showed any more and I felt quite confident that I could get myself on a bus and back to my own house without significant mishap. My father would be at home, which meant that it wouldn't look odd my going straight to my room and shutting myself away, something I knew I'd have to do to avoid my mother's keen gaze. I had been expelled from school for using cannabis: the deputy head, a nun called Mother Sylvester, had come to our house and explained that I was a hopeless dope fiend and had to be removed for the common good, then she'd handed my mother a leaflet in which the most obvious signs of drug use – dilated pupils, very small pupils, talkativeness, reclusiveness, loss of interest in hygiene and personal appearance, etc. – were carefully set out. Luckily, my father was on back shift for that episode in my continuing education, and though he knew I'd been expelled, he didn't find out why until much later. It can be a real blessing, sometimes, to be the child of an indifferent parent.

On the bus ride home, I sat with my face pressed to the window, gazing out at the passing landscape, great oaks shrouded in gloaming, lights coming on in the stone houses along the way, rabbits hurrying out to feed in the half-dark. As the bus approached Great Oakley, I saw a fox crossing a field – and it might have been around then that an absurdly impractical notion began to form at the back my mind. People were always asking me, then, what I was going to do with my life and I'd never known how to answer that question. I knew I didn't want to become a *professional person* and I didn't think I wanted to go to university, but I'd never come up with even the remotest notion of what I *did* want. Now, in some vague way, I was beginning to imagine that, while I had no strong idea of how, I could become a witness to the world I had entered that morning, a world made sumptuous and bright like an Alfred East painting. I was confident, now, that the acid had more or less worn off, and I could tell that I was thinking lucidly because I was still sufficiently aware of my own ineptitude at drawing to know that I would never be a painter. But I reckoned that I *could* become a photographer. All I needed was a decent camera and the state of grace that I had just discovered would write itself out in silver and light. At that moment, I could almost see the pictures I would make: they would be like nothing anyone had ever done before, I decided, not because they would be particularly original, in a technical or artistic sense, but because they would create a record of the sumptuous quality of everyday things, as seen by someone on a permanent acid trip – and, as clichéd as this idea sounds, at that moment I thought I had come up with something extraordinary. Gazing out at the streets flowing by – the bus had now entered the first of the Corby housing estates – I decreed that I would be a photographer on acid and the first pictures I took would be of people's houses, in all conditions: in daylight, at night, in rich suburbs and poor schemes, in the local area to begin with and then, later, when I had more money, in other places. California. Buenos Aires. Dakar. Houses seen from the air, or from passing trains; empty ruins and rich mansions; mud huts, hovels, yurts, tepees, cabins. I would start by photographing the exteriors, then I would go inside and take pictures, not of the people, but of the things they owned, the marks of wear and use those things left behind, the shadows they cast. The quality of existence: that would be my only objective. I would find the line that divides mere objects from whatever it is that makes transcendent beauty part of the fabric of the world and I would photograph it. I suppose, at the back of my mind, I knew that none of this would actually happen; but at least I had a purpose, for the time being. Something to do. A pursuit. A pastime.

The Ensign Ranger was an awkward camera for a beginner, but I couldn't afford anything else. It would have been easier if I could have bought an SLR 35mm and carried it around in a fancy camera bag, the way my friend Bob did, but Bob had money and I didn't and, besides, I liked the look of the Ensign, I liked the fact that the lens was on a bellows, that you had to use a cable release to work the shutter, and, before long, I was a passionate devotee of the larger format 120 film which, in the hands of the accomplished photographer I thought I would quickly become, would give the kind of results I was looking for. I didn't want crispness, I didn't want hi-tech, I wanted depth of focus and I wanted a sense of suggested detail. I didn't want to go in search of the decisive moment – by the time I got myself set up, the decisive moment would already have been far in the past – and I didn't want to take pictures in colour, not because black and white was more artistic, but because I was after a notion of drab – rainwater dripping from a line of raincoats in a village hall, say, a local image that would convey the universal, that all across Illinois, or Russia, it's raining on grain stores and wrecking yards, just as it is raining here. By now, I wasn't thinking of myself as an artist, in the usual way; I wanted to be an archivist, or something of that order. The pictures I took wouldn't make sense unless they were viewed en masse: one image leading to another, a narrative that spoke of class and privilege and injustice building up over the space of hundreds of images. My first project was a neighbour's house, a two-up two-down end-of-terrace home indistinguishable from any other house on the estate, and I used several rolls of film on it, sometimes on acid, sometimes not, but I quickly became dissatisfied with that, and for a while, unable to find my way into what I thought of as my major project, I switched to self-portraits. I'd been looking at photographs by Diane Arbus and August Sander and Paul Strand, and though people as such didn't interest me very much, faces did. What was missing, what was masked, what was yet to come – these were the interesting things and, because I didn't think of myself as a person, I began taking pictures of my own face. Moving from the Ensign to a Voigtländer – it was said that this was the only camera that the Emperor of Japan would allow in his presence – I began experimenting with lighting and backgrounds. I can't imagine who I thought I was, in my narrow box room under the eaves of my mother's house, taking pictures of myself with a self-timer and a tripod, and I have no idea, now, what I hoped to achieve. Some of those pictures had me lit from below, so I looked like a monster or a demagogue, some were lit from above; most, however, came out as mere snapshots, revealing nothing but a decent likeness. One day, as I returned from a developing and printing session with Bob (who was so well-off, he even had a makeshift darkroom), my mother caught sight of the bundle of pictures in my hand and asked if she could look. I didn't want to let her see, I already knew how ordinary they were, but she was quite insistent and eventually I gave in.

'They're all of you,' she said.

'Yes.'

'Why's that?'

I didn't answer, but watched in silence as she leafed through the images one by one, lingering over some, passing quickly over others.

'I don't know why you have to take stuff like this,' she said, not showing me what she was looking at, though I could guess. 'This doesn't even look like you.' She moved to the next picture, while I waited; then, her face breaking into a smile, she pulled one of the photographs from the pile and held it out for me to see. 'This is a good one,' she said.

I looked. It was an ordinary snapshot, a fair likeness of someone that, from the inside out, I didn't even know. Yet, at the same time, I had to admit that it was a fair likeness. Physically. In the cold light of day. 'It's all right,' I said, reaching a hand to take back the stack of pictures.

My mother let me have them, then, but she held on to this one. The one she had chosen. The one she liked and wanted to study further. 'Do you know who this looks like?' she said.

'No,' I said. I thought she was going to tell me I looked like my Uncle Tom, her smart brother, or maybe even her eldest sister, Eleanor, now long dead, who had once been a schoolteacher and had been revered in my grandmother's house like some old-time saint. I certainly assumed that it would be someone from her side of the family, and I was surprised when she disappeared for a moment, then came back clutching the Egyptian handbag – a gift from my father when he came back from a tour of duty in Palestine – where she kept all her treasures. Snapshots, family documents, all kinds of ephemera and tat. She didn't have to look very hard, so she must have known where the picture she wanted was. It was an old, careworn image of a boy about my age from the late thirties or forties, and it looked exactly like me, as I was then, in 1972, in the picture I had taken of myself – but I didn't know who it was for a long moment. Then, to my horror, I realised.

My mother smiled and put both pictures away in the Egyptian bag. 'Don't tell your dad,' she said.

FIFTH DIGRESSION:
ON MURDER BALLADS

At about the same time I started taking pictures, I graduated from Catholic Club discos to the more or less grown-up dance halls around town. The Nag's Head and the Raven were the best of them and, pretty soon, everyone that mattered would be out dancing at the Nag's on a Saturday night, and if they weren't there, they were sure to be at the Raven. By everyone, I mean the warm-blooded folks, sixth-formers and factory girls in their party best and those bright, careless boys who wandered in from the various estates, full of romance and banter, boys who danced, thinking it was the girls they were after, though what they really loved was the music and the night, and a faint, local sense of wonder that sometimes kicked in when you least expected it. Those boys were true gentlemen, in the old sense: they knew the words to the songs, they actually liked the girls and, because they were just out to play for the evening, they didn't have any specific intentions. Their banter could be pointed but it was innocent of malice and, at heart, they knew they were far less guileful than they pretended.

These boys had friends, but they were essentially alone on the dance floor, and that made them vulnerable, because the ones who didn't dance worked in packs; like stray dogs, they were a variety of local biohazard, a source of possible contamination that couldn't be avoided – and nobody wanted to catch their eye. They never danced, they didn't even drink that much, they just stood hawking at us from the sidelines and waiting to make something ugly happen. It took me a long time to work it out, but eventually I came to understand that the pack dogs hated the dancers not so much because they were jealous of them, but because they were mystified and embarrassed, like some rube at a carnival who, unable to work out how the trick works, lashes out at the sideshow magician. They hadn't come to play; they were out to claim proprietorial rights over something, or someone. They might claim one particularly bright individual, a dancer who, making his way to the bar, hadn't shown them the exaggerated respect they merited, and that would be ugly for a moment (a jostle of elbows, a spilled drink, a glass or a bottle smashed in the dancer's face), but far uglier were the drawn-out, niggling campaigns of threat and mockery directed at certain couples – chosen, it seemed, for reasons only the pack mind could figure out. It was dispiriting to watch as two people came together, in the sway and heat of some classic Motown tune, lit up from within by a surprised pleasure at finding themselves glamoured by the moment, and then to see the pack move in, the victims pressing bravely on, like people on a first date at some new restaurant on the wrong side of town, outdoor tables and coloured lights in the trees for that touch of magic, but no escaping the attack dogs barking and snarling in the windy scrapyard, just ten yards away.

I was never sure if the pack boys knew how much we despised

them. Admittedly, the whole scenario was fairly second-rate, all bad frocks and boys trying to look like Rod Stewart, but there were still times out on the floor when the dancers were glamoured, in spite of their cheap outfits and pallid, factory-hand looks, because you could see they were living for the moment, inside the music, and not giving any sort of a damn. On the other side, the pack had no glamour at all, just a dull afterglow of raked-over ashes and the pit-dog stare that you had to turn away from, not only because it was frightening – and it was frightening, because there were always more of them than you – but also because you recoiled, instinctively, from the possibility of contamination. Everybody knew that to return the stare was considered an act of aggression; but we also knew that, once the non-dancers had chosen their mark, there was no avoiding them anyway. The protocol was juvenile: *What are you looking at?* one of the pack boys would say, the conventional response being, *Nothing*; at which point, before the innocent civilian could find some form of words to explain away the unintended insult, it was all over. Even when the dancer knew something was coming, it was usually too late; the inevitable winner in this type of confrontation is the one who is prepared both to strike first and to do the most damage. In pack-dog-world, it doesn't matter if a man is strong, fast or quick-witted if he has not viciousness. As in business, say, or local politics, victory goes to he who most lacks scruple.

As the alternative initial query – *Are you screwing me?* – makes clear, this kind of attack is also psychosexual, reminding us where the real joys of pack-dog manhood lie. I once worked with a sales director (pack dog with pinstripes) whose entire vocabulary operated on the same basis – *These guys are screwing us; Do we want to get into bed with these people?; We distract him with this, then we come up quick and take him from behind*, and, after one particularly disastrous presentation, the unforgettable opener: *I was stark bloody naked out there, and they were just lining up to fuck me.* It's an ancient mystery, but still a puzzling one, that a certain breed of human male draws his best analogies for random violence from the physical act that ought least to resemble gratuitous assault. This has nothing to do with the Chinese description of sex as 'flowery combat' – in which play is of the essence – because it is devoid of play, just as it is devoid of drama. *Are you screwing me?* is a question that can come only from the kind of person who either stays off the floor altogether or comes lumbering in at the end of the night to *make his move* – proof positive that he doesn't *get it* and, in all likelihood, never will. On the other side, doing the best he can to ignore the pack, the dancer is completely exposed. At his best, he lives by native wit and a rare mix of energy and caution. Innocent of bravado, he finds in himself a vein of real wildness, a vestige of the dancer spirit that, in old myths, could halt even the greatest of warriors in his tracks. That was all illusion, no doubt, but in our planned community New Town, if you hadn't learned by the age of sixteen that illusion was all you had, then you were stuck with nothing at all, other than a smart mouth and an exaggerated sense of self-righteousness.

Because it is so frequently perpetrated by the (physically, or politically) strong against the (physically, or financially) weak, the readiness to take part in everyday violence is ugly and routine, a character flaw that originates in the sense of having been 'shaped in iniquity', an all too obvious lack of some inner Narcissus, expressing itself in random and tawdry attacks on whatever unsuspecting victim might happen along. Pack boys; husbands and fathers with 'quick hands'; moneyed insiders flushing every last cent from a pension fund, because it's so easy, like taking candy from a baby – they're all the same, all secret self-haters in spite of the swagger and the braggadocio, and they got that way, not because Mummy didn't love them, but because they cannot even begin to love themselves. They can be charming and charismatic; given their advantages, they can they even dazzle and, sometimes, like Lord Arlen, who murders Mattie Groves in the old ballad after he finds the commoner in bed with his wife, they may even go through the motions of honourable combat and cry, *It will never be said in fair England / that I slew a naked [i.e. unarmed] man.* But then, honourable combat, like the law, is always rigged in the richer man's favour: the aristo and the pleb fight with swords, but though Mattie does his best, he is no match for someone with Arlen's education in swordsmanship. Still, as honourable as he pretends to be, this lordling is thoroughly despised by his wife, who clearly had good reasons for inviting Mattie into her bed – and when she is told to choose between her husband and her dead lover, she immediately rejects the unlovable Arlen (interestingly, though this nobleman sees it as dishonourable to slay a naked *man*, he has no such scruples about a defenceless woman; but then, the lady is, after all, his wife and therefore a mere chattel):

And then Lord Arlen he took his wife,
He sat her on his knee
Saying who do you like the best of us,
Mattie Groves or me.

And then spoke up his own dear wife
Never heard to speak so free
I'd rather a kiss on dead Mattie's lips
Than you and your finery.

Lord Arlen he jumped up
And loudly he did bawl
He stuck his wife right through the heart
And pinned her against the wall.

No one is completely innocent in the ballad tradition, but it is clear that this example (a variant on Child Ballad 81, 'Little Musgrave and Lady Barnard') pits the wayward and the impulsive against the power system for good reason, and though, like Paolo and Francesca, the lovers are doomed from the start, the old, natural, pagan impulses that motivate them are clearly preferable to the conventional, property-based code of the privileged. In other words, this is a song about the class struggle that says, no matter how privileged you are, you cannot command love.

The origins of the 'Little Musgrave' ballad are unclear, but it was not uncommon for murder ballads to draw on real-life, or supposedly real-life, criminal cases. 'Pretty Polly', for example, takes the bare bones of its story from a broadside ballad ('The Gosport Tragedy') describing the murder of a local girl by a 'cruel ship's carpenter' after he learns that she is pregnant; 'Frankie and Johnny' was inspired by press accounts of the murder of Albert Britt by his lover, Frankie Baker, after Britt won a slow-dancing competition with another woman. Even when their source is the gutter press, however, the ballads succeed in transforming their material into haunting, strangely glamoured narratives: as Rennie Sparks, of the Handsome Family, has remarked, 'The first time you hear "Pretty Polly", you giggle nervously. The dark forest flowing with blood, the beautiful girl, the open grave; it makes you dizzy with a strange mixture of horror and delight' – and I have to admit that there were times, outside the Raven or the Nag's, in an aftermath of blood and sudden quiet, when a curious, dark variety of delight did compete with more predictable feelings of pity, or horror. It was rare, this delight, and it was beyond rational justification; nevertheless, there were moments when something elemental seemed to have taken place: a chill, upward swell from the undercurrent that flowed through our workaday existence, some memory of a *thrawn* pagan narrative that, while it could never cancel it out, might, on occasion, obviate the miserly logic by which we normally lived, a black, sticky glamour that, as ugly as it might seem, was still more vivid and persuasive than what we had learned to think of as *normal*. It was a borrowed glamour, of course – something we would have seen differently, had our usual lives been richer – but it made for a sense of narrative and, like the killing of Annie James, it was *our* narrative, and not something imposed on us by some development corporation or planning committee. Under certain circumstances, circumstances wholly independent of the moral and human aspect of the scene, these narratives could seem inevitable, bewildering natural events like heath fires or flooding, painful to witness, but true and, given the base facts of existence in that place, as near to tragedy as we would ever come.

The best interpreters of the murder ballad recognise this quality of the inevitable, adding just a touch of extra shadow to the killer's bewilderment at the crucial moment: he doesn't know why he committed his crime, there is a sense that he hadn't set out to do actual harm and, now that the inevitable narrative has run its course, he is as mystified as anyone. The telling is often quite matter-of-fact, the narrative of someone in shock, or possibly resigned to his fate; often the killer will not ask for pity or mercy for himself, but will be transfixed by the image of his victim. To take just one example: in Dock Boggs's version of 'Wild Bill Jones' (arguably the best murder song of all), the narrator tells how, having found Wild Bill walking and talking with a girl he considers his own true love, he pulls out his pistol and impulsively shoots the twenty-two-year-old who considers himself 'too old to be controlled'; but it is the way he describes the death of his rival that makes the song so powerful:

> I drew a revolver from my side
> And I destroyed one poor boy's soul.
> He rambled and he scrambled all on the ground
> And he gave one deathly moan.
> He looked in the face of his darling true love;
> Says, 'Oh darling you are left alone.'

– and it is no great stretch of the imagination to suggest that, as he observes this touching exchange between Bill and the girl, the killer tacitly recognises the strength of his victim's love as greater than his own. What is of the essence, however, is the simple fact that nobody here knows why this is happening, or how to prevent the loss of one poor boy's soul, or the moral destruction of the other. People do not choose to act in the murder ballads; things happen of their own bewildering accord. It's a frequent theme: the Beloved is rejected on a whim (in 'Barbara Allen', for example, sweet William is condemned to a lonely death for having 'made the healths gae round and round / And slighted Barbara Allen'), or murdered for any number of reasons, some of which can be formulated in terms a jealous lover can understand (*If I can't have you, nobody will* or, as in the case of 'Pretty Polly', *We had some good times, but I'm a rambling man and I'm not about to settle down*), though the most interesting, to my mind, is that most perverse of variants – *I want you, but I don't want to want you, so you have to die.* The best example of this is probably 'The Knoxville Girl', where the narrator kills his lover for no given reason:

> We went to take an evening walk
> About a mile from town
> I picked a stick up off the ground
> And knocked that fair girl down
>
> She fell down on her bended knees
> For mercy she did cry
> Oh, Willie dear, don't kill me here
> I'm unprepared to die

She never spoke another word
I only beat her more
Until the ground around me
Within her blood did flow.

He then goes home, covered in blood, is arrested and taken to prison:

They carried me down to Knoxville
And put me in a cell,
My friends all tried to get me out
But none could go my bail,

I'm here to waste my life away
Down in this dirty old jail,
Because I murdered that Knoxville girl,
The girl I loved so well.

I still remember the first time I heard this song. It should have been a curiosity, nothing more, but that wasn't how I saw it that afternoon, dogged off from school and sitting in a friend's living room while his parents were away, drinking cheap rum and listening to the Louvin Brothers' *Tragic Songs of Life*, which he'd found in his father's record collection. I'd never heard the Louvin Brothers before – that kind of music wasn't easy to come by back then – but I was fascinated, especially by 'The Knoxville Girl'. It should have struck me as histrionic, or needlessly perverse, or, at the very least, a murder ballad that had just gone too far, but it didn't – and I didn't see it as cruel or malicious either. I recognised the condition it described and, though I felt both the horror of the crime and pity for the young victim, I understood that, for the man in this song, the regard of the other, her loving, entangling gaze, had become too much to bear. To be looked at can appear as a challenge to anyone, under different circumstances: the pack dog is so crudely put together that even a passing glance is interpreted as an act of aggression but, because honest self-regard is such a taboo in a society that, to keep us docile, must keep us guessing about our self-worth, we all have our limits. So, because I understood that at some level (though nowhere near as consciously as this sounds), I didn't see the murder as a literal event: this song wasn't the account of a true crime, but a kind of warning. A cautionary tale. However, for reasons that I was too young and unsuspecting to understand that afternoon, it was a warning that seeped right into the core of me – and instead of hearing what it said and moving on, some backwater in my mind chose to give it permanent lodging.

WELCOME TO THE MACHINE

(*Pink Floyd, 1975*)

I didn't want to do the whole higher education trip, but because I had no ambition to do anything else, my mother persuaded me to apply to one place, and if I was accepted, I would agree to try it for a year. With no other plans on the table, I didn't have much to argue with, so I sent off an application to the Tech College in Cambridge, quite confident they wouldn't take me. When they did – I'd managed some pretty lacklustre grades, though apparently not lacklustre enough – my mother was delighted; she didn't know the Tech wasn't a proper university, like the places my smarter cousins had attended, she just heard the word Cambridge and let her imagination go to work. Meanwhile, I was no better informed. All I really knew about Cambridge was that Syd Barrett lived there with his mum, and that Grantchester Meadows was a short bike ride from the city centre. Other than that, I assumed it was a bunch of rich boys wandering about being clever and preparing themselves for government and the planning of New Towns for us plebs. Still, I'd made a deal, and when I saw how happy she was, I knew I would have to stay the course to the end if I could; so, in the autumn of 1973, I moved out of my mother's house and, other than weekend visits, a couple of summer jobs at the Works and a five-month spell keeping house during her final illness three years later, Cambridge was my new home.

I don't remember much about college. Three years came and went, I read books that had nothing to do with the courses I was taking and spent every free minute in the Arts Cinema on Market Passage. I imagined myself in love three times during the first two years and, on each occasion, brought to the affair the kind of theatre I'd learned from Jean-Pierre Léaud in all the French movies I'd seen at the Arts; then, in my final term, I actually did fall in love and, though the young woman in question was almost unbearably beautiful, funny as hell and highly intelligent, I was bewhaped by the whole experience and emerged no wiser than before. When my mother fell ill, not long after finals, I went home to look after her but, as soon as the funeral was over, I went back to Cambridge, found a menial job and rented an old caravan that was parked in the backyard of a pub, my only companion the landlord's dog, a large Rottweiler whose name I have now mercifully forgotten. Every time I returned from the city centre and opened the gate to our shared domain, the huge beast greeted me with a series of deep, sinister growls that seemed to rise from a primeval darkness in its chest. I imagine the gate was intended to protect the general public from this obviously disenchanted creature, though it did nothing to protect me. It almost goes without saying that the Rottweiler and I didn't get along; though I confess, the fault was as much mine as it was his. By then, I didn't get along with anyone, or even any *thing*, other than a handful of inanimate objects that I had gradually become accustomed to using. A fountain pen, a dozen or so books, an old skillet that I'd bought in a junk shop, surprising myself with an unexpected streak of practicality; these, and a few other items, were my true companions, the presences that made my narrow, single-berth caravan into an approximation of home. Truth to tell, however, my ideal place, the place where I might have felt truly comfortable, would have been an impossible limbo of white space and silence, interrupted only by the occasional flit of a bird shadow across a wall, or a thin, almost imperceptible strain of music; one of Britten's String Quartets, perhaps, or a very distant phrase from a Debussy prelude. Yet, though I know now, and probably suspected then, that this was nothing more than romantic affectation, during those eighteen months before I met Christina, I fancied myself as something of a recluse. My favourite reading matter was Rousseau's *Les Rêveries du promeneur solitaire* (other favourites included Stendhal, Faulkner and Proust, which I read doggedly and very slowly in French: perhaps half the pleasure was that my limited comprehension of the texts suggested a happy, but rather cloudy world that I could barely make out, and to which I would never be admitted). My favourite times to be out of doors were dusk and dawn, when I would pursue my own solitary promenades around the outer reaches of the city; my meals were monastically simple, with carrots and plain boiled rice the most regular items on the menu. At one point, I decided to live on a diet of granary bread from Basil's bakery and rollmop herrings; I stuck to that regime for several weeks, then switched to nothing but milk (with disastrous consequences, it has to be said), before turning at last to a more varied diet of oatcakes, tinned asparagus and

Portuguese sardines in brine, each breakfast, lunch and dinner accompanied by a set quantity of weak Darjeeling and a sliver of lemon. The idea was to become as light as possible, not physically so much as in one's inner self; by which I think I meant, not the soul, but the shadow body that lives inside each of us, the fat or thin man struggling to get out, the secret dancer or swimmer that we cannot hope for on the outside but see, so clearly, in the chambers of our imagery. The idea, already recognised as an impossibility but no less fervently pursued for that, was to become capable of flight. Part of this project, as with all my projects at that time, was to be alone for as much of the day as I could. Glenn Gould used to say that everyone has a 'solitude quotient', and that his was particularly high, but, at twenty, I would have made that maestro of lonely nights and self-medication look like a social butterfly. I lived like this for a long time, alone in my little world, eating raw vegetables and poring over books in a language I barely understood. Then, without warning, everything changed.

The owner of the Rottweiler was a plump, moustachioed man of around fifty called Ron, but most of my dealings were with his wife, Irene. Every Saturday morning, after I'd fought my way past the Rottweiler, the custom was that I would go into the kitchen at the back of the pub to pay my rent and Irene would always have some gift from her smallholding (a bag of home-grown tomatoes, say, or a bowl of eggs) laid by for me; then, as soon as the money transaction was concluded, she would take me through to the lounge bar and pull me pint of Abbot Ale, so that I felt more like the prodigal returned than a mere lodger. One Saturday morning, however, there was no bowl of eggs, and no tomatoes, and Irene was sitting at the table very calmly drinking a cup of tea. Or rather, my first impression was that she was very calm; I later understood that she was in shock.

'Good morning, Irene,' I said. 'I've brought the rent.' Behind me the Rottweiler was still pawing at the door and growling. I have no idea, now, how I ever got past him.

Irene looked up at me from what seemed an impossible distance. 'Oh,' she said, 'don't worry about that . . . There's no rent this week . . .' She rose slightly from her chair then sat down again, and now I saw the sadness in her eyes.

'How do you mean?' I asked, for want of something better to say.

'Well,' she said, 'Ron's gone off. Don't know where, but he's gone for good, apparently.'

I stared at her, dumbfounded. The way she said it had been so matter-of-fact. I scarcely knew Ron, but he didn't seem the type to just up and leave. Or was he? The only exchange of conversation I remembered having with him had concluded inexplicably with the words: *Well, in my experience, there's only one thing worse than not getting what you want.* I couldn't remember the context, and it had seemed like nothing at the time, just a touch of wry humour; now it suggested malice aforethought. 'Gone off?' I said. It was as much as I could muster.

I didn't learn the full story till much later. Ron had run away with a twenty-five-year-old barmaid named Ellen and most of his wife's savings, leaving her with the pub and the smallholding – and the Rottweiler. Irene didn't tell me this that Saturday morning, she just repeated that Ron was gone, she didn't know where. 'And that's that, I suppose.' She smiled. 'Would you like a cup of tea?' A week later, she came out to the caravan and told me she was very sorry but I would have to find somewhere else to stay, she was giving up the pub and the smallholding – which I knew was the big love of her life – in order to move to Lowestoft, where her sister had a nice villa by the sea. As she was telling me this, tears came to her eyes, and though they were probably occasioned by the thought of having to give up her chickens and her vegetable plot, I think they were also partly for me.

'I'm really sorry, Irene,' I said, as she refused once again, that last day, to accept any rent. 'I had no idea –'

'Of course you didn't,' she said. 'Why would you? You only saw us at our best . . .' She smiled. 'We kept up a pretty good act, over the years.'

'A good act?'

'Yes,' she said. 'We did pretty well, all things considered. I can't speak for him, now, but I was proud of how well we did. We'd got so we were experts at just going on as if everything was . . .' She gave me an inquisitive look, as if I might step in to fill the gap. I guessed what she wanted to say – *hunky-dory*, *the cat's whiskers*, some phrase from my mother's era that masked the ordinary malaise of workaday life. The marriage. The shared property. The silences when something ought to have been said, or all the talk when silence was the only decent choice. And under it all, the tacit refusals of touch and memory.

She nodded, then, as if she had read my mind. 'I suppose that's what actors do, isn't it?' she said. 'When they're in a play that runs for years. *The Mousetrap*, that kind of thing. How long has that been running now?'

'What?'

'The Mousetrap?'

I didn't know, but I hazarded a guess. 'Ten years?'

'Oh no,' she said, 'it's much longer than that. And I imagine they get bored doing the same thing every night, but they take great pride in making it seem . . .'

'Fresh?' I ventured.

'More than that,' she said. 'Like they are delighted to be doing this one thing, the one thing they have always wanted to do with their lives.'

She was still standing at the door of the caravan; now, suddenly remembering my manners, I asked if she wanted to come in. She shook her head and made a move to go back to the house – and that was when I noticed that the Rottweiler wasn't there growling at us. 'Where's the dog?' I asked.

'Hm?'

I tried and failed to recall the Rottweiler's name. 'Where's, um . . .?' I looked around the yard.

'Oh,' she said, 'he's gone. I gave him to a friend of . . .' Her voice trailed away and I understood that she didn't want to say Ron's name. 'He's such a fool,' she said, after a moment's silence for the dog. 'He says he loves her, but that's ridiculous. I mean . . . Surely it's not about that kind of thing any more. Not at our age.' She shook her head sadly, but there was no bitterness when she spoke again. 'That girl will take him for everything we owned,' she said. 'I don't understand why he doesn't see that.'

Another, longer silence fell as we bowed our heads and considered Ron's folly, while I tried to remember which of the barmaids I'd seen around the place was Ellen. Was she the pretty one, with the shoulder-length blonde hair, or the one with the mole on her cheek and dark ringlets that made her look like some latter-day Moll Flanders? Either one seemed out of Ron's league, but then, I couldn't really imagine Ron with anyone, though before I could stop it, the irreverent thought that I would have gone for Moll crossed my mind. I looked up. Irene was studying me with a penny-for-your-thoughts expression and I forced my mind to go blank. She gave a little nod, acknowledging some thought or memory that had just passed through her head, and it struck me how elegantly she was dealing with this farce. I would have been tracking Ron through the wilds of East Anglia with a baseball bat or a machete – not for love, you understand, but for the money. 'I saw it once,' she said, her voice brightening.

'Saw what?' I asked.

She was smiling again. '*The Mousetrap*,' she said.

PIANO

In spite of myself, the insidious mastery of song
Betrays me back, till the heart of me weeps to belong
To the old Sunday evenings at home, with winter outside
                                            D. H. Lawrence

Early in the summer of 2009, driving north over the Forth
Road Bridge, with the car radio set to some Golden Oldies
programme, I remembered that my mother didn't exist any
more. I have been crossing this stretch of water for half a century,
from the days when it was almost black, with just a scatter of
silvery inklings from the pub and house lights of the Queensferries
to show that anything was there at all, to the brilliant gantries
and rigs of this present season of incessant commerce – and,
more often than I have chosen to remember, this crossing has
brought me back to memories of her. This, I should say, has
nothing to do with maternal water imagery, or any other such
Freudian show-and-tell: it's not that kind of narrative. No: the
image that forms in my mind is precise and, for once, it's not
about me, or my psychological problems. It's about her.

I loved my mother. To some, this might sound like a statement of the obvious, but the actual fact is that this affirmation

141

is hard-won. Hard-won, because I also blamed her – for remaining with the disastrous husband she so clearly and inexplicably loved, for being in thrall to Priestcraft and convention and Holy Mother Church, for not taking an interest in the great books and the politics that came not just to obsess me, growing up, but also to seem the sole defence against an unjust world. Back when the only bridge over this firth carried our train from Cowdenbeath to Auld Reekie on occasional shopping trips, my father would dole out halfpennies to my sister and me, so we could toss them into the firth and make a wish. My mother hated that. She hated to see anything go to waste, because we had so little in the first place, and that would upset all of us, because our shared extravagances were so few. There were times, later, when it seemed that everything she did and said was designed to bind me further into her world of church and home economies, a lone creature locked into a sleep of milk and privet like the enchanted child in some old fairy tale, barely awake and coddled in the slow, maternal sepsis of simple faith and social class. Clearly, there are many ways to cast your spell.

My first memory of her is in the kitchen at King Street on a winter's morning. The windows are streaming with condensation and she is leaning into my face, her perfume sweet and a little too damp. She is singing to me, but what is surprising is that the song is 'A Gordon for Me', a tune I normally associate with my father, who would sing it when he came home drunk from the club. Why is she singing that song? I wonder – a song she must have associated, for the most part, with unhappy times, my father's breath soured by whisky, the housekeeping money gone, and her having to put on a face and pretend nothing was wrong. Maybe it was a way of having him there with us, as he should have been, on some family occasion that he had missed – my birthday, maybe, or their wedding anniversary. Other memories have us walking on the Cuddy Road, going out into the open country around our pit town for miles, climbing barbed-wire fences and fording tractor-wheel puddles, or sitting by the radio, listening for the good songs.

Later, a few months after she died, when I was too stupefied by grief to accommodate such memories, I put her out of my mind. Haunted for years by my father's incompetence and worried that, one day, I would see his likeness gazing back through a mirror, I forgot her inner strength and her shy ability to cope with the sorry detail of an almost untenable daily round. I am ashamed, now, to admit it, but it's only during the last several years – a time in which I have grown older than she ever lived to be – that I see her clearly again, not as the salt-of-the-earth, indefatigable working-class wifie I would paint her as for my middle-class college friends, but as the young woman I once believed was the most beautiful person in the world, the woman who taught me to read from hand-me-down magazines and then, later, to bake, our Saturdays given over to sifting flour and peeling apples in the fogged kitchen of our prefab on the edge of Cowdenbeath, while my father drifted across town between the pub and the bookmaker's, frittering away what money he had earned that week on whisky and the ponies. Flour, dried peas and lentils, potatoes from our little garden plot and volunteer raspberries from the verges around disused fruit farms – until my mother broke with tradition and found a job of her own – these were our staples, along with the eggs our neighbour, Mr Kirk, gave me for helping him with the chickens, and occasional scraps from the butcher who kept shop at the foot of Stenhouse Street in a cool, tiled space hung with new carcasses, the sweet blood falling, now and then, to form dark pearls on the sawdust floor. I have always loved butchers. I love their craft and I love their acquaintanceship with steel and flesh, but, more than this, I love them for the kindnesses shown to my mother in that little shop, for the bones and scraps they set aside for 'Tess' to carry home for a dog that never existed. It's no cliché to say that my mother was a proud woman, but she also had children and, with a profligate casual labourer for a husband, there were times when she had to ask for, or silently accept, a kind soul's charity. That said, she never sacrificed one iota of her innate dignity: she didn't play hard done by, she didn't flirt, she never tried to pretend she didn't know what was happening – and she treated everyone as her equal, in every circumstance, no matter how much richer or luckier than us they might have been.

Now, when my mind goes back to this younger version of her (partly to counter memories of the living ghost she became before she died, at forty-seven, from ovarian cancer), I know that, if everyone were to live as she did, the injustices natural to a class-based system would not only continue, but proliferate. I believe, with Emerson, that every actual state is corrupt and that the only counter to the cynical self-interest of the weak and the greedy in the 'higher' echelons of society is constant vigilance and, until it is possible to storm the temple and over-turn the moneylenders' tables, a preparedness to kick against the pricks whenever the opportunity presents itself. By now, it is impossible not to see that the poorest are being cheated every day of their lives, sometimes in the most surprising ways, and it would be wrong to adopt the kind of quietist stance my mother would have advocated. Still, I wish I could have learned from her, along with the books and the baking, some element of that art she had of treating everyone with the same respect she would have accorded a miner, or a factory worker. For too long, I have harboured the bitterness of the societal underling who knows he is smarter than his masters – and that bitterness came from my father, a labourer all his life who was ten times more intelligent, though infinitely less cunning, than his foreman. It has been a heavy gift, and hard to carry, but I cannot blame him for it, for I know all the ways he was harassed and frustrated by the world, and we should not judge the one who falls when it is clear that everything was stacked against him. All I can do is wish that he had been strong enough to keep his bitter gift to himself and let his children go out into the treacherous world empty-handed, as my mother did, ready to make good, ready to ask for a moment's grace and ready, should that moment present itself, to share it with whosoever happened to be present.

A time comes when the inner life is mostly about memory. The great loves and hurts are in the past, as are the hopes and prayers, and now it is a matter of lingering on the quotidian, on the fine detail where the true order of things continues, insignificant and essential as the bloom on a plum or the cracked varnish of an Imari bowl in some old still-life painting. I think that time came early for my mother and I seem to recall that there was a period – quite short, perhaps a year or two – when she rebelled against having everything, or what must have seemed like everything, taken away from her. She would have known, at some point, that she had married the wrong man and, though that knowledge would have taken some years to become final, she must have reached the conclusion, eventually, that she had made a mistake that could not be corrected. Divorce was possible in those days, of course, even for a Catholic, but it wasn't within my mother's purview: where she came from, a woman married for life and stood by her husband, no matter what. Besides, she had children and I don't think she was able to contemplate making them suddenly fatherless. I didn't doubt that, had she pushed him, my father would have walked away from us all, and I came to the conclusion, sometime around my twelfth birthday, that we would have been better off without him. She would never have left him, though, and I knew that, too. Her bed was made and she was lying in it.

Every now and then, however, her heart would lift and she would find some reason to be happy. The trouble was that, for her, happiness was supposed to be inclusive. She wanted to share the good moments, she wanted to look across a room and smile at someone, knowing they were glad as she was glad – only my father always refused to be that person. Whenever she fabricated a moment's quiet or contentment, he would shrug it off, or wave it away, angry, it seemed, to be offered something so meagre, in a world that owed him so much. At the end of his life, I think he came to understand the pain he had caused, but I don't think he ever knew that *this* was what hurt her

146

most, this refusal to be happy with her, if only for a moment, in an unfair world. Yet it *was* what hurt her most and, eventually, she stopped trying and withdrew into her own inner place, a curious half-smile on her face and a distant look in her eyes, as if she were gazing past us all to something we couldn't see. For a time, I felt sad for her, when she drifted away from us like that, sad and also excluded because, like any child, I was afraid of not knowing what my mother was thinking, afraid that she might disappear altogether into the inward sanctuary she had created. My sister was even more frightened by this and, sometimes, when our mother slipped away into some dream we could not see or hear, Margaret would cry and pull at her sleeve till she came back to us – which she did without complaint or any show of impatience, simply rising from her chair and going on with what she had been doing, as if to reassure us that everything was normal.

I have no idea what she thought about or dreamed during those absences, but I know she drew strength from them – and as the years passed, and we moved away from everything and everyone she knew and loved, I watched her develop a keen ability to illuminate her world, and ours, by tiny yet significant acts of imagination, transforming an afternoon when my father was away into a minor feast day, adding touches of colour or music to our lives, or learning new recipes and cooking them for us in our ugly kitchenette (my father's tastes ran no further than meat and potatoes, in some form or another). Nothing about Corby pleased her, or us: it was a grey industrial town divided by sectarianism and tribal resentments, but she made the best of it and I learned to admire the quality of her imagination. She lasted another decade in that place, during which time she came to accept the affection of new workmates and neighbours, who came every day during her long illness with flowers and news from the big world, baffling my father with their kindness. Through it all, she was more interested in how they were doing than in her own condition: she knew she was dying but wouldn't admit it, because she had guessed that my father was concealing that fact from her, and she knew he couldn't cope with bringing it into the open. Sometimes, when I sat with her through the long evenings, she drifted into the other-world she had created and, when she returned, I saw a new, if fleeting, light in her face as she turned to find me there, almost wondering who it was before she realised I was her son. Then she would ask me to bring her something so that, this small chore done, she could assure me she was all fine for now and send me away to live my own life for a while.

I cannot say that I know what it is to be a man, but anything I learned about being human I learned, in the first instance, from my mother. We are all born with our own gifts and these can be a curse or a blessing, but what we learn, if we are lucky, are abilities that become virtues insofar as they temper our natural character. My father's gifts to me were anger against injustice and a certain volatility that, at its best, makes me impatient with easy answers and received ideas, and this impatience can sometimes stumble into original thinking. Too often, however, I slide into pointless rage and, more regularly than I would like, I am the kind of man my father was: remote, disgusted by the world, self-righteous and given to violent imaginings. When I let her, however, my mother's ghost comes with her workaday bravery, her respect for others and her gift for filling the gaps in a damaged life with small acts of the imagination. If my father made me a man, with all the flaws and clumsiness that entails, then my mother countered him by teaching me to be human, and an artist, after my fashion, as she was after hers. Nothing is perfect, she says, but as much as my father's ghost rails against that imperfection, hers assures me that what is to hand is, or can be, enough and I try, as well as I am able, to believe her. That said, there is another side to all this that has to be acknowledged. Any virtue, taken to extremes, can become a fault and, all through my teenage years, I was endlessly amazed by my mother's readiness to accept the status quo. It wasn't resignation; it wasn't simple defeatism; she really did manage to persuade herself that some unseen justice was at work, when other people were chosen for all the good things in life, and she was left with the dregs. To the rest of us, the rich and the powerful were cheats: born in the right place, to the right parents, at the right moment, they walked among us as privileged, confident beings, bright and highly functional like lovely machines, and their sole task was to hang on to what they had by making sure that nobody else got a taste. We, the unlucky ones, were bewildered by this, but we understood *misfortune* instinctively. It seemed logical to us that bad things happened, and though we very rarely saw them coming, we understood, afterwards, that they were inevitable. My mother's plan, however, was that I would be different. I would be the fortunate son. The lad o' pairts. She had the entire narrative mapped out: a catalogue of prizes and achievements, professional standing, a nice Catholic wife. Further on down the road, this vision included a large house with children and a car of my own – and to be fair, if you came from the places she knew, these were good and honest aspirations. Out in the workaday world that she mostly feared, policemen with torches and long sticks were criss-crossing a stretch of moorland, searching for the latest murder victim, drug addicts were begging for pennies on street corners, a gang of men were beating another man unconscious in the car park of a local pub. As far as she was concerned, the only way to avoid all that was to become a lawyer, or a doctor, or maybe a teacher in a college, a person respected in the community, buffered by money and regard – and as I sat by her sickbed, in the summer of her forty-eighth, and my twenty-third, year, I felt real grief that the choices I had made, or failed to make, had added to the marrow-deep disappointment that was now killing her. It was July 1977; Donna Summer was number one in the charts with 'I Feel Love' and, somewhere in Whitehall, the closure of Corby steelworks was being quietly organised, bringing a planned end to the planned community to which we had reluctantly migrated twelve years earlier.

I was living in my mother's house for the last time, working in the same factory she had worked in before she became too sick to carry on. That bothered her more than anything, even more than the pain she suffered every day, but I couldn't figure out how to tell her that my failure to accomplish the dream life she had planned for me wasn't deliberate. Had I been capable of doing so, I would have signed up for law or accounting, curried favour with the bosses, mortgaged myself three times over for the nice house in the suburbs where she would come and make fairy cakes for her grandchildren. I wanted to take out a photograph and say to her: *Look, this is Amanda with the girls, there's Alice throwing a stick for the dog, here's Emily on her new bike.* But I couldn't – not because I had no opportunities for social advancement, but because, at that time, and probably still, her ambitions for me would have demanded tacit collaboration with a social system that, even if I escaped it, would continue to grind down people like her and my father.

I had nothing against money (although I did feel it should be more evenly distributed, and any argument against doing exactly that struck me as specious, cowardly or self-serving, depending on who advanced it). Still, growing up poor in Cowdenbeath and then in Corby, I had been horrified by the existence of the rich. When they passed me on the street I would experience a faint rush of disgust. There was an etiquette to such encounters, of course: my mother would tell me not to *stare*, so I would look away very elaborately, while the rich people – an elderly couple in expensive overcoats, say – averted their eyes in much the same way, though their reasons for doing so were different and their disregard seemed so natural as to be an involuntary reflex. Sometimes, I even thought that my mother and I were invisible to them – or, if we did skim across their radar, we appeared as a separate species, whose lifelikeness was in some doubt. Which was odd because, to me, they were the ones who seemed less alive: in fact, I could never quite shake off the notion that wealth was secretly and intrinsically in league with death. At school, I had learned that animals are unaware of their own mortality – they live in the moment, and have not guessed, yet, that they will some day die – and on the rare occasions when I caught the eye of a rich person, it seemed to me that they suffered from the same ignorance.

Of course, when I say *the rich* here, I mean those moneyed folk who moved and had their relatively expensive being in my small world: people who dressed well and drove expensive cars, people who had their own businesses, people who went out in fur coats and jewellery to mayoral dinners at the town hall. To the very rich, these people would have been mere specks, but to me they were strange monsters, steeped in privilege and capable of breathtaking, if utterly civil heartless-ness. And yet, while I felt affronted by their existence, I did not envy them their possessions and I had no desire to be *like* them. I savoured the things that belonged to me and I knew, if I were given the choice, I would rather be me than anyone else. As lucky as they were, as wholly as they defined the world I had to inhabit, I would not have changed places with a rich man's son, because that would have meant assuming a different – and to my child's mind, an inferior – subjectivity. Who would happily become someone else, I reasoned, if that someone else did not feel and think like himself? Nobody else would hear music as I did, or see the colours I saw. Nobody else could dream my dreams or think my thoughts – and what point could there possibly be in being someone who did not think and dream and see and hear exactly as I did? None at all; and by this tortured logic I arrived at something close to detachment. Close to, but not quite. True, I did not want to be one of the better-offs, but

I hated them for depriving my mother of the modest house on a quiet, leafy street that she knew all her life she would never have, the house she dreamed about when we went for walks in the 'nicer' parts of town, she and I peering through gates or over cast-iron railings at the wide, empty lawns, the clipped hedges, the doors left open to the summer sun that led into the deep, sumptuous interiors that rich people took for granted.

For several months, then, I worked shifts at the factory and occasionally ran around town with a girl called Lizzie, while my mother lay dying in the mingling scents of her own wasting body and the regular bouquets of summer flowers from her friend Beryl's garden. As her body failed, her mind grew fiercer, in spite of the drugs, and she said things that she hadn't been able to say before. All the same, I knew she was holding back on the one thing she most wanted to say. By then, I had created a vision of her death, one that I found bearable, in which she lay daydreaming in her morphine shroud, recovering a single happy moment from the past, like some random snapshot found between the pages of a book, a single moment of light and specific colour to slide into before the gold of this world goes to shadow. That wasn't the story that death had in mind for her, though, and I think she spent the last several days trying to find a way of saying something that she probably knew from the first couldn't be said. I don't know that for sure, of course, but after the misunderstandings and evasions we had all lived through, she and my father and their children, what would she have wanted, other than to ask those she was leaving behind to love one another? Or if not love, then, at least, look after. It's only now that I begin to understand how difficult it must have been, knowing that she couldn't realistically make that request.

Bitte betrachten Sie mich als einen Traum! This remark of Kafka's, delivered during a visit to his friend Max Brod, appears to have been completely spontaneous. 'Please, consider me a dream,' he said, when he inadvertently disturbed Brod's father, a banker, at work in his study. In all her forty-seven years, my mother never read a word of Kafka, but she would have appreciated the beauty of that saying: to be no more intrusive than a dream, to have the freedom from imaginary riches that a dreamer has, to live in a world that has its own, incorruptible logic, all of this would have appealed to her. To actually become a waking dream, however, is a somewhat more complicated art than self-effacement and the ingrained asceticism of the merely pious. To go about one's business and leave no trace, to be the adept who owns nothing but has the use of everything, requires extreme discipline and consummate imagination, and it is nothing more than an evasion, merely to own nothing, it is nothing more than an evasion, merely to leave no trace. We have to go about our business and make use of what we find in the world, as we find it, according to the logic of a will that is not defined by social convention, but by its own nature. I can't speak for Kafka, but it seemed to me, that day, that my mother had glided through her life like a dream by choosing to forgo that logic, living on almost nothing in order to be no trouble to those around her – and, as her life came to an end, I wished desperately that she would demand something more. I wanted her to die, not as a dream in the life of others, but as herself, allowing the anger and bitterness and justifiable contempt to emerge and finally dissipate – though at the same time, I understood that she was incapable of such an impropriety.

MISS YOU

(*The Rolling Stones, 1978*)

After moving out of Irene's caravan, I spent the next year or so flitting from one place of lodging, and one menial job, to another. Now that my mother was dead, I had no further reason to go back to Corby; I had no reason to go anywhere, in fact, so I didn't. I just drifted from pub to pub, and party to party, doing anything I needed to do to stay afloat. In such inner dialogue as went on, there was no further reference to love; good Catholic boy that I had been, I was now blinded with the wisdom that everything was sex, no matter what the radio said. Sex, drugs, parties, music you could dance to – and enough money to get by, without being part of 'The System'. Stay light; keep moving; beware of gifts, plans, attachments and other forms of possession. That sounds corny and seedy, no doubt, but in its own way (and with all due respect to Rube Bloom and Harry Ruby) a not entirely dishonourable version of the simple life. Soon, the only people I knew were people I'd met in pubs.

Which is where I met Jack Williams. On the kind of summer's day that no longer happens, our paths crossed in the yard of the Panton Arms, which was situated, once upon a time, on a side street near Parker's Piece, in a city that no longer exists. Of course, there's still a Panton Arms in Cambridge, and there's still a Parker's Piece, but the city from which Jack and I drifted together that day (from the Live and Let Live, in one direction, and the Eagle, in the other), a city I once knew like the back of my hand, really has gone and in its place stands a perfect, empty simulacrum that nobody who ever crossed the Piece or made his way along Mill Road in the late 1970s would even begin to recognise. By which I mean: to *recognise*, in the way one country recognises another, investing it with credibility and political status, and being recognised, in turn, as something equally real, and equally tentative. I arrived at the Panton around twelve thirty, looking for a paunchy, crossword-obsessed biker-type who sometimes provided me with Methedrine. Jack came in about twenty minutes after, which he did pretty much every day (as I later found out), because it was a convenient place to end up at lunchtime closing, just a few minutes from a flat on Lensfield Road where he was welcome, under almost any circumstances, to while away the afternoons with music and booze and vague, wandering conversations till the pubs opened again at six. Jack was somewhere around twenty-three. A stick-thin, beagle-eyed man with a straggling Jesus beard who bore a passing resemblance to the 13th Floor Elevators' Roky Erickson, he always dressed in the same Levi jacket and straight-leg jeans, and there was something both charming and sad about him, the way he seemed alone in even the largest crowd, the occasional old-fashioned turn of phrase he would use, and, most of all, the sense he had of himself, for reasons he never shared, as being bound to an idea of courtesy that, had he not carried it so well, would have seemed merely pretentious. He didn't work but he always had enough money; apparently his parents, who divided their time between Brussels and London, paid him a generous allowance to stay far away from them for as much of the time as was decently possible. He spent that allowance on beer and dope and the occasional pie, which he ate slowly and with obvious reluctance, in one or other of the various pubs he frequented. Late at night, when he passed out at a party, someone always covered him with a blanket; when he woke up next day – always earlier than anyone else – he would make tea for whoever was there, whether he was in his own house or not.

Mainly because my friend hadn't shown by closing time, I fell in with Jack that day, and then, over the next couple of weeks, with his friends – and that was how I met Christina. I didn't actively choose to be part of this group – I was adrift, nothing more, a piece of flotsam ready to attach myself to anything with sufficient gravity to hold me for a while – but there was something about Jack's friends that made them seem not so much attractive as exempt, for a summer or two, from the usual laws of existence. Most of the time, they played games of various sorts – Pooh Sticks on the river, table skittles at the Blue Ball in Grantchester, Frisbee on Parker's Piece – and when they were playing, they were extremely likeable. They were charmed, and they knew it, but this only made them all the more easy-going – and if at times they wanted something better, some sense of gravity or some more perilous foray into the dark side of the fair, they didn't linger over the thought for long.

That first afternoon was typical. After a few beers, during

which we forged the easy acquaintance of male souls with enough alcohol in their blood to feel well disposed towards the whole of creation, Jack and I sat under a lime tree on the Piece and smoked some grass, before wandering round to his friends' house to pass the time till the pubs opened again. It could have been anywhere, that well-appointed flat on Lensfield Road, and it could have been any day of my life. If I hadn't been there, drinking white wine and listening to Van Morrison, I would have been somewhere else, doing something similar. But it *wasn't* just any old day, it was the first afternoon of a summer that would soon lead me to a faraway and hitherto uninhabited parish of the imagination lit with Chinese lanterns and scented with the slow green of the river.

That wasn't obvious on the first day, however, when Jack brought me to meet his friends, a pair of near-identical, though not twinned, sisters from Minneapolis named Kristen and Julie, and we sat all afternoon with the windows open, drinking icy and not inexpensive Chablis and drifting in and out of conversation, everyone strangely disengaged, not quite stoned, not quite drunk, just going along in a pleasant, amicable haze with the summer heat and the sounds drifting up from the street below. Every now and then, Julie would leap up and go into the kitchen to freshen our drinks, but Kristen remained motionless in what was obviously her favourite place on the sofa. Clearly the spoilt child of the family, she was two years younger than Julie, a carefully distant nineteen-year-old all wrapped up in her own world – and if you hadn't met anyone like her before, she would have seemed unimaginably cool, not likeable so much as admirably indifferent, so that, when you were with her, nothing seemed to matter, other than the moment and the incontrovertible judgements that she never pronounced, as such, but which were all too obvious in the way she turned her head, or smiled, serene as a cat and pointedly *other*. One step short of pretty, with a flat, rather wan face and thick, ash-blonde hair, Kristen was one of the coldest people I have ever met and I recognised that immediately; but then, I have always been drawn to cold, the way cattle are drawn to one of their number lying dead at the edge of a field, staring a while in wonder and bewilderment before moving away to other things, haunted only briefly by the mystery they have witnessed. It pains me now to admit it, but to begin with, it was this chill girl who captured my attention. Somewhere at the back of my mind, I may even have considered entering into some doomed affair, but the notion quickly passed, and long before Christina turned up, I had abandoned the idea of that cold romance. I can't say for sure, but I think that annoyed Kristen somewhat. Of course, I had seen right away that she didn't want a *romance*, or not as such; she was, in fact, a more than usually asexual instance of the ice-maiden type, and I couldn't have imagined her ever touching, or being touched by, anyone. Still, she seemed to like the idea of my being hopelessly in thrall to her and she didn't want, quite, to relinquish the attention – so much so that she was prepared to sabotage any promising friendship that I might strike up with some pretty gap-year student I met at the Panton, or the stoned English rose with whom I spent a single enchanted hour at a party out in the suburbs, an hour I remember to this day, mainly, perhaps, because it went no further. Kristen saw to that. And though I wouldn't want to attribute any other

motive than self-involved game-playing to her in this matter, I
must also confess that Kristen's manipulations served me rather
well, because, at the time, I really had no desire to get into a
romance that might involve even the least degree of reciproca-
tion. What interested me, in fact, was another kind of game
altogether – a game that might be referred to as Blue Angel
Syndrome, for want of a better term – and if I didn't play it
with Kristen, it was only because she was too obvious, and
probably too shallow, a candidate. I needed someone who,
unlike Kristen, *could* have touched, and could have *been* touched,
under the right circumstances. In short, I needed a Christina
and, even before she arrived at Lensfield Road, just two weeks
after I did, I knew, in my own befuddled fashion, that she was
already on her way.

The past is very rarely visual for me. Yes, I see images and I
remember certain places quite vividly, but when I hear someone
tell a memory that sounds like a scene from a film, I am mystified. For me, memory – for the most part – is like a narrative
I read, or heard tell of somewhere, an account; visually, it's a
series of stills, at best, though, more often than not, it's a handful
of blurred snapshots accompanied by a gloss, the outline of a
scene, rather than the scene itself. The night I met Christina,
however, is a perfect piece of cinematography. It had been a
hot day and I had been in a stuffy classroom for hours (I'd
somehow got a fixed-length part-time summer job teaching
English as a foreign language to a lively band of Italian teen-
agers); now all I wanted was a drink, and by the stroke of six,
I was in the Panton, nursing a beer and waiting to see who

would show up first. Inevitably, it was Jack, but it wasn't long before most of the gang were there – Harry, Jim, the rich kids Neil and his brother Tom, a precocious newcomer named Paolo, who looked about twelve years old but drank like a fish, a sixth-former called Jacqueline-not-Jackie, who was Neil's latest girlfriend and a couple of girls from Cherry Hinton whose names were Tess and Maddy, though I could never recall which was which. It wasn't till around eight, though, that Julie came in, explaining that she couldn't stay long because she and Kristen had a guest, a friend from Minnesota, though we were all welcome back at the flat whenever we felt like drifting over. After she left, we lingered a while, having surmised that the new arrival would need some time to settle in; then, at around ten thirty, people started getting it together to head out – and that, as it happened, was when my chubby biker friend showed up with what he invariably referred to as a 'package' for me. Everyone in that group smoked dope, and some of them may have been into other things, but I was cautious about scoring Methedrine in front of them, so I told them to go ahead and I'd come along later.

Which I did, quite soon, but by the time I arrived, the flat was quiet. When I got to the door it was so still I didn't even knock, but stood a moment to listen, thinking that no one was there, that they'd heard about some party on the other side of town and headed off without me. Not being inner circle, I wasn't somebody they would have made a point of waiting for, and I knew that – but after a moment, just as I was about to turn away, I heard a sweet, solitary sound from inside the flat and I knew someone was there. I stood dead still and listened: it was the sound of a flute being played – not a record, definitely not a record. It was being played very well, but I knew right away that it wasn't coming from a machine. It was the sound of someone who, suddenly gifted with an unexpected moment of solitude, has taken out her instrument and started to play, enjoying the still and the quiet, and the sound she makes echoing in a strange and, for her, unknown place, a flat in Cambridge, England, as opposed to wherever she came from, a place where she could be herself and no one but, doing what she loved doing most. I say this, not because of what I learned about her later – it has nothing to do with hindsight. I simply knew what she was doing and who she was, and I stood a while, listening as she played, only bringing myself to knock on the door when she broke off, halfway through a phrase from a piece I had never heard before. There was a brief silence, then a body came to the door and I found myself standing face to face with what I believed, at that moment, was the most beautiful person I had ever seen – and, though I remind myself that I'd just done a significant amount of Methedrine in a very short space of time, it is a belief I still cannot entirely dispel.

She was medium height, with warm, brown eyes and very dark, almost black hair, someone you would call pretty, or even a little *too* pretty, if you weren't paying attention and didn't notice the energy coming off her, the slight, but undeniable sense that here was someone who could barely contain herself, someone who dwelt, all the time, at the edge of some wild, possibly dark, but not at all unfriendly or dangerous place – and liked it. She was wearing a dark blue sweatshirt and faded jeans, and she was barefoot – I noticed this somehow, even though I wasn't aware of having looked at her feet. I knew right away that she was alone in the flat, and I suspected, without knowing why, that she had been glad of that. Still she didn't seem to mind the intrusion, and though she'd probably expected to open the door to someone at least vaguely familiar, she was untroubled by the fact that she had found a complete stranger instead. At the same time, I was also aware that I was still on that first sweet rush that comes of doing a couple of lines of meth back to back, and that it probably showed.

'Hi,' she said. 'You must be John.' She stepped back slightly, to indicate that I could enter. I nodded – and, again, it must have been obvious that I was racking my brain, trying to remember her name. I was sure Julie had mentioned it at the Panton, but it had gone clean out of my head. She laughed. 'I'm Christina,' she said. 'And you should come on in. The others won't be long.'

Sadly, she was right. But the next several minutes – ten, fifteen maybe – still run through my head like a loop of Super 8, a little grainy from time, perhaps, but clear, and in sequence and, most surprising of all, for someone like me, precise to the smallest detail. I can see, now, the slightly amused expression on her face as she invited me in, the way she crossed the room – in that flat, the front door led to a large, bright kitchen with views over Lensfield Road – and started to clean and put away the flute she had just stopped playing. I hear the sound of her voice, that soft, beguiling Midwestern accent; I see again the way she turned her head to look at me, then looked back to the flute in her hand and how, at that moment, she had the look of a woman in a Dutch painting, all the available light seeming to fall on her and single her out, as if by some occult attraction. The conversation was polite, superficial: the others had gone out for tobacco and papers, leaving her to practise; she had to practise every day, no matter how tired or jet-lagged she was, or she would slide into bad habits; she was a friend of Julie's from Minnesota, which I already knew; she and Julie had stayed in touch, writing letters and visiting from time to time after Julie moved to England. I asked her how long she had been playing the flute, and that led to my asking – trying to seem nothing more than polite and, at the same time, to let her see that it meant more to me than I was pretending – if I could hear her play sometime.

'But you've heard me play already,' she said. She closed the instrument case then and everything stopped for one dizzying moment. Then she looked at me – and there was a suggestion in that look, a merest, faint flicker of a suggestion, that she wasn't just being polite either – and she smiled. 'But I have a piece I've just learned that I think you might like.' The way she said it left no doubt that she understood something was happening on my side of the room – I had only come a few steps into the kitchen – and that she didn't just find my predicament amusing. For a moment, it almost seemed that she would take the flute out and start playing again, right then and there, but before either of us could say or do anything else, the door opened and Kristen came in, clutching a bottle of wine. And though she preceded the rest of the gang by only a moment or so, it was obvious that, in the space of those few seconds, she had read the situation unerringly – even though there really *was* no situation, outside my own fancy and the sense of a lingering pause on the air that must have suggested a possibility that, for a spoiler like her, could not be allowed to unfold. She looked at me. 'You made it, then?' she said. She said this so sharply that Christina came close to wincing; then she laughed. 'Be careful of this one,' she said. 'He's not as helpless as he seems.' Then the rest of the gang tumbled in and started moving about the kitchen, a single, half-drunk entity, some fetching glasses, others opening bottles, while Neil – who, more than anyone, had the run of the house – went to the music system in the corner, fished out a Spike Jones record, and put it on. A moment later, the room was filled with the sound of 'Cocktails for Two' and I knew that, whatever it was that had passed between me and Christina before they arrived, none of them, other than Kristen, had noticed a thing.

It's not the first love that counts, or the second, or even the last, according to Jacques Chardonne. What matters is the love that folds two separate destinies into the flow of common life.[29] I can see, now, that this is a fine notion, but at the time I met Christina, I was as far from *la vie commune* as it was possible to be. Not that this is really much of an explanation for my behaviour over that summer, behaviour that was cruel, childish and stupidly perverse. I imagine, if there is to be any explan-ation, that perversity – mine and, to some extent, Kristen's – is

[29] '*Ce n'est pas le premier amour qui compte, ni le second, ni le dernier. C'est celui qui a mêlé deux destinées dans la vie commune.*' (Jacques Chardonne)

the main culprit, but I have no doubt that fear also played its part. The question that remains, however, is where perversity ended and fear began. I wasn't ready to be in love, not like that, and the boyish soul in me was repelled by the idea of something that actually *mattered*, something that made everything else conditional. So it comes as no surprise that I woke up miserable and confused the morning after that first meeting with Christina – no, more than that, I woke up in a blind funk, because I knew, or rather, I was trying to avoid recognising that I knew, that the logic of the little sex and drugs and rock & roll world I had constructed was now irrevocably different. Now, the premise of Christina's existence was the single most important factor in that world's logic – and this was a situation I very much wanted to avoid. If this all sounds like a man clutching at straws, it's because I am. More than thirty years after the fact, I am still trying to figure out what happened that summer. I am still trying to understand why I did what I did, and I have no answers, easy or otherwise. I tell myself that some events just defy explanation, but I don't ever quite believe it.

According to Elizabeth Bishop, losing is an art that 'isn't hard to master', and though I believe this is true (after all, as Bishop points out 'things seem filled with the intent of being lost'), I also believe that the before and after of this solitary discipline, that is, the preparedness to abandon or be abandoned and the inventiveness needed to celebrate that loss, are both more difficult to put into practice and significantly more rewarding. To invite, and then celebrate, that moment when the entire world seems, in the words of Pablo Neruda, 'forsaken like the docks at first light',[30] calls for a particular sensitivity to the differences between the romantic and the sentimental mode. To master the art of losing, we must be willing to consider ourselves lucky when whatever god we address answers our prayers by refusing them, so that something more interesting can happen.

Yet while anyone who has ever been forsaken knows that to lose artfully is infinitely preferable to the squalid business of trying to win back what is already gone – the near-hysterical farce of what might be called Don't Leave Me This Way Syndrome – it is also the case that all things must pass according to their season – *a time to get, and a time to lose; a time to keep, and a time to cast away* – and though the time to lose will come, the gambler's urge to cast everything away on a whim is best resisted. Losing is an art form, yes, but throwing it all away, *Nashville Skyline*-style, is nothing more than a gesture, a refusal motivated by fear, rather than by artistry, or by the irregular grammar of *amour fou*. The act of throwing it all away, no matter how nonchalant it seems, is an act of desperation born of the knowledge that we lack the know-how or the strength or the imaginative depth to keep something – which is to say: to take responsibility for, to maintain, to have and to hold.

There is nothing very interesting about romantic love. Not for others, at least. Without Shakespeare's wit, *Romeo and Juliet* would consist of two choreographed fencing matches and the Queen Mab speech; without Iago, Othello's 'light-wing'd toys of feathered Cupid' would have us drowsing in our seats – or

[30] '*abandonado como los muelles en el alba*'. (Pablo Neruda: *La Canción desesperada*)

rolling in the aisles. I could try to describe the emotions I experienced over the days and weeks I spent in Christina's company (though rarely *with* her, as such), but it would doubt-less sound like the lyrics to some old pop song – and, even allowing for *that* degree of hyperbole, nothing I said would come anywhere near the breathless, awed sense of the other I experienced whenever she and I were in the same room. That sense of the other that erases all the trivial and distracting nonsense of the crowd, and of the self's all too frequent inward monologue of interminable doubt and second-guessing. All the clichés apply: whenever she was present, everyone else faded to backdrop, extras in a corny film where the camera is intent on following the star's every move; every time she smiled, it was me she was smiling at, or for; every time she opened her mouth to speak, it seemed that it was *me* she was addressing, no matter who else was present; on the few occasions when the rest of the gang drifted away and we were left alone, I felt as if I were standing at the edge of a precipice, waiting to fall – and I knew that I could fall at any moment, simply by reaching out and touching her, or blabbering some witless declaration of love that would have left the seventeen-year-old Romeo groaning with embarrassment. But – and here is the difficult part, because this is utterly inexplicable – the *but* in all this, the stumbling block, wasn't that I knew, or thought I knew, what Kristen had told me that first evening, after she had noticed the tension between us in her kitchen – a story about Christina's previous visit to Cambridge, when she and one of the inner circle, a painfully shy, likeable boy called Eddie, had formed some kind of attachment. It wasn't that, and it wasn't shyness, or hesitation on my part that held me back. Not at all: if I could have frozen time long enough to gather myself up and make a decision, I would have betrayed Eddie in an instant, and even though I *was* shy of Christina – not of anyone else, only her – that shyness wasn't enough to explain my endless, strangely delicious hesitation. Some of the difficulties I experienced were occasioned by the mere presence of *the others* – by now, the entire gang seemed one single, homogenous, endlessly irritating mass – and, at the time, I let myself believe that the regime of constant interruption they imposed was the main problem. It was only much later – so much later, in fact, that my lack of self-awareness embarrasses me, even now – after Christina was gone, and everything was lost, that I saw how I alone had been the real obstacle to whatever might have happened that summer. It wasn't Eddie, it wasn't the others, and it wasn't shyness. It was perversity. The truth is that, as the summer unfolded, I ventured further and further into a strange, twisted maze of desire and refusal that eventually had nothing to do with Christina at all. It was an ugly, self-absorbed game that I had been waiting to play for years – a game for one, no matter how many might seem to be involved, a game that only I recognised, in retrospect, as Blue Angel Syndrome in its cruellest – and so, most exquisite – form. I didn't formulate it in so many words, but now I can say that this was the way out of my funk of that first morning. Christina existed, yes; her existence was unbearable, yes; but I was fine for as long as I played that game of longing and refusal. I had been in love before, or thought I had, but this was the first time I'd experienced all the clichés of *amour fou* – emotions and sensations that I had always thought of as absurd, symptoms of a self-induced hysterical condition that had more to do with florid imaginings than with an actual response to another flesh-and-blood creature. All that summer, I couldn't stop thinking about Christina; her face, her smile, her voice were at the back of my mind all the time, and even when I drifted into merciful, usually alcohol-induced, reverie, she was in my dreams. The only excuse for how I conducted myself is that I knew how ridiculous the situation would become if I allowed it to continue along the conventional, boy-meets-girl lines that my inward heart so desperately wanted to pursue.[31]

The memory of that summer – or rather of the three weeks or so during which this game played out – is something that I will never lose and a shame I can never live down, because there is no way to make amends, there is no explanation to be offered. What saddens me now, when making amends isn't even remotely an option, is the sheer effort and inventiveness I expended on pushing Christina away. I had some help: the hapless Eddie was always present, merging into and out of the wallpaper, a constant spur to my conscience – and of course Kristen proved to be a formidable ally. After the first evening, she watched me like a hawk and fed me lies and half-truths about Christina and Eddie's secret history; meanwhile, whenever Christina was around, Kristen would discreetly shepherd Eddie towards her. She put considerable effort into having me believe that something really had gone on between these two the previous summer,

---

[31] '*Le désir fleurit, la possession flétrit toutes choses.*' (Marcel Proust)

but if it had, neither seemed to remember it as vividly as Kristen did. There was no doubting the fact that Eddie was a man in love – and with the encouragement Kristen was providing on a more or less daily basis, he might have believed that something wonderful was just about to happen – but Christina treated him with little more than fond and bemused tolerance. Meanwhile, I was playing my own game, the game that was supposed to rescue me from utter confusion. Every time Christina walked into a room, the world stood still; a strange new gravity had come into existence, a pull that made me want to touch her – and the more I wanted this, the more effort I put into staying clear. If she looked at me across a crowded room, I looked away. If she spoke to me directly, I became cheerfully vague or evasive. I longed to be alone with her, but I knew that, if I were, I would have nothing to say. Not that saying something was what the situation required. What was required was touch, a moment's contact that could not be gone back on.

So it continued, the whole gang eddying back and forth across town, mostly together, sometimes leaving stragglers behind for a while, though if it was one of the inner circle, a Ben or a Neil, say, we would wait till they caught us up again. The most moneyed of the group, Neil and Tom, were both qualified hot-air-balloon pilots, and occasionally they would disappear for a weekend and float off into the empyrean like the Montgolfiers; when they returned, there would be a certain light, and a touch of ozone to them, that served them well when they trawled for sixth-form girls and foreign-language students in the various pubs around town. Meanwhile, Jack had started to eat even less and drink more, for reasons that nobody could have explained, even if they had tried – though they didn't try, they just moved in closer, like herd creatures trying to shield one of their most vulnerable from some unseen predator. The more I saw of them, the more I understood that they weren't just a circle of friends, brought together by a fondness for alcohol and childish games; that inner group was more like family, a wandering gaggle of near-siblings, bonded and defined by the absence of something that money and youth couldn't outweigh, the well-dressed inhabitants of a hypothetical orphanage on a day trip to the city, with enough pocket money to make it seem magical. They were a family, a community, and by a kind of circumstantial default, they belonged to one another – and because she was Julie's closest friend from childhood, Christina was one of the inner circle. I, on the other hand, stood at the periphery – and that may also have played some part in the proceedings of that slow, hot summer.

Eventually, things had to come to a head. That sad dance couldn't last forever and, though I was intent on going on as if nothing out of the ordinary was happening, I knew something had to give, sooner or later. One evening, after we had all punted up the river for drinks at the Blue Ball, I left the pub alone and started walking across the Meadows, following the river back towards town. I had slipped away on the quiet: I was becoming increasingly irritated by Kristen, with the way she constantly steered Eddie into Christina's orbit, but I was also apprehensive because I was beginning to weary of the game I was playing and I knew – I was afraid – that I might give it up at any moment. Having sneaked away successfully (so I thought), I was happy to be out on my own, away from the cigarette smoke and the noise.

'Hey!' The voice came from ten yards back in the soft, smudged-charcoal gloaming, but I knew who it was right away. 'Wait for me, won't you?'

I didn't want to stop, but I did. When she caught up with me, Christina smiled brightly and we fell into step and continued on, the river to our right, a perfect haze of a summer's evening gathering around us. Neither of us said much for the first part of this walk; she was pretending that she hadn't followed me out of the Blue Ball and I was pretending the same thing, all the while wondering if anyone had seen her go. Yet, in spite of the quiet between us, this was a dangerous moment. I kept glancing at her, idiotic notions running through my head, that strange gravity pulling me towards her. At one point, she slipped her arm into mine and walked in step with me for several paces before she sensed what she presumed was discomfort, or embarrassment, and drew away. She stopped then, and looked out across the river to where the cattle were watching us. It was something they did: if you walked up through the meadows in the evening, they would gather in groups of five or six and track you along the opposite bank, hurrying forward then slowing again, not quite keeping pace, always adjusting, but watching your every move with a kind of puzzled curiosity.

'I wonder what they think we're doing here,' she said, as the cattle came to a halt opposite.

I didn't say anything. I just stood gazing at her like an idiot, remembering the second poem I ever memorised in school:

Byron's poem that begins 'She walks in beauty like the night'. God knows why they get children of twelve or thirteen to memorise poems like that. Unlike the first recital piece I had learned for assembly – Edward Thomas's poem that starts *Out in the dark over the snow / The fallow fawns invisible go / With the fallow doe* – I hadn't understood a word of it, or rather, I had, but I'd thought it silly, comparing a woman to the night, just as it was silly to say my love is like a red, red rose (which only made me think of sunburn, or blood), or to suggest, in this country of all places, that one could be lonely *as a cloud*. Now, all of a sudden, years after I'd gone up onstage under the watchful gaze of the drama teacher and run through those lines like they were items in a shopping list, I felt the full power of that poem, which I could still remember and which, annoyingly, began to run through my head as we stood there staring at the cows. *She walks in beauty like the night*: it was true, no matter how corny it sounded and, as the poem continued in my mind's ear, I saw, for the first time, that Byron wasn't just following some convention, like a Tin Pan Alley lyricist churning out a three-minute hit, he actually meant what he was saying, even down to the last line, the one I had always doubted most: *A heart whose love is innocent*. Was Christina's heart innocent? Was mine?

'And what are *you* thinking about?' Christina asked.

I looked at her. Everything was going wrong: proximity, eye contact, that gravity pulling us together, but I couldn't do anything to stop it now, and even if there were no words, the look happened, and then the touch and then she was pressed close to my body, my arms around her, our mouths almost touching. Even then, I still think it could have been stopped, but one of us kissed the other, it is hard to say who, and then we stood, holding on in the near dark, while the cows lost interest in us and drifted off into the field beyond.

INTERLUDE: SMILES OF
A SUMMER NIGHT

(*Ingmar Bergman, 1956*)

It's a summer's night. You are alone in the house, or perhaps
there are others, somewhere nearby, but they are sleeping in
their own beds, locked away in the virtual world, leaving sole
possession of the here and now to you, a reality that is somehow
more real at times like this: no distractions, no interruptions,
every given thing laid out around you, steeped in its own order,
its own fine textures and shades. At first, you feel you should
be doing something – there's work to catch up on, or there's
been so much work that you need to relax in some recognised
way, with a bottle or a book or a TV screen – but after a while
you slip into limbo, an in-between and so slightly altered state,
not just of the mind, but also of the flesh. It's a condition not
unlike hypnagogic reverie, that halfway house between waking
and sleep where dreams unfold into the light of day and are
transposed, for milliseconds, into a reality that is more real than
anything else you know. At the same time, you are almost bored:
aimless, free of preoccupation, you drift from place to place,
studying the everyday objects you take for granted, or going
slowly through the motions of some familiar task that, subject

to this new attention, is suddenly transformed into a precise and rather beautiful rite.

This is a game, of course; or a thought experiment, perhaps. The task is to imagine yourself in this condition and, then, in the course of some ordinary, and now seemingly magical, routine, you cut, or burn, or crush a finger, or the palm of your hand – a minor injury that, ordinarily, would be nothing more than an inconvenience. Only, tonight, alone in the house, in this condition of reverie, you choose not to see it as such. You don't grab some kitchen towel to mop up the blood, you don't run the burnt hand under cold water, you don't release the trapped finger from wherever it was caught. Instead, you linger on the pain, letting it happen, letting it unfold into a fullness that you usually avoid. There are times when this pain would be annoying, or distracting, but tonight, for a minute or two, and maybe even longer, it becomes something else, something eerier, something glamoured. Experienced under these conditions, there is, in this pain, a real and actual pleasure – and after you have experienced this pleasure-in-pain several times, the idea that it could be shared starts to seem, at the very least, feasible. Of course, you understand from the beginning that it is not something you could share with just anyone – and that raises questions you had never thought to ask till now, questions about love and trust and belonging, questions about the difference between ordinary romantic love and *amour fou*. Without wishing to, you begin to divide your lovers, past and present, into those with whom such a moment might be shared, and those for whom it would be, quite simply, inconceivable. It should be stated clearly, here, that this division alters nothing – or not in the usual run of things.

Outwith this limbo state, in the world of waking and ordinary dreams, you feel no more or less love, or remembered fondness, for those on one side of the dividing line than you feel for those on the other; this is simply a matter of categorisation, like hair or eye colour, or tone of voice. And yet, for this glamoured moment, everything is altered. You know that what happens here has no impact on your other, run-time life – it belongs entirely to this night's particular limbo; but you also know that, with the mere recognition of that romantic division, your world has been enriched, its shadows deeper, its highlights brighter, an old chiaroscuro recovered from the depths of your limbic system. I say recovered, because this is how it happens: you didn't know what you had, but it was always there, and you suspected something of the kind all along. You could have gone through your whole life without finding it and, more often than not, the act of recovery is incidental, an accident of sorts, a matter of seeming chance. Now, though, you are in another house and, even if you run for your life, slamming door after door behind you, you can never quite forget that you have been there. And that house, in turn, never forgets its visitors. If, for some reason, you cannot learn to return to that house, with care and attention and the skills of a master cartographer, it will come back to haunt you, in the ordinary day-to-day, and there is no telling what harm you might do.

RUNNING AWAY

(Bob Marley and the Wailers, 1978)

I always like it, in the old movies, when the lovers move in to kiss or make love and the camera lets them go, surrendering them to the dark and to their privacy, on the one hand, and to the delicate territory of imagination on the other. I never wanted to intrude upon that moment, most especially on the first embrace. After Cornelia Parker wrapped a mile of string around Rodin's sculpture *The Kiss* (in which a nude couple embrace, though their lips do not touch), she said: '*The Kiss* used to be considered indecent. People thought it should be covered up, which in effect is what I've done. I don't think I have hidden the eroticism. If you conceal things, they become more charged.' *The Kiss* was originally part of a larger sculpture, *The Gates of Hell*, and was intended to depict Francesca da Rimini and her brother-in-law, Paolo Malatesta, the adulterous lovers who are tossed and blown about in the storm with the other lustful souls in Dante's *Inferno*. The two had fallen in love while reading the story of Lancelot and Guinevere, but when Francesca's husband, Gianciotto (John the Cripple), discovered the affair, he murdered them both.

Now *there* was a kiss that both parties would have taken back, if they could, but a kiss cannot be erased; once it happens, everything changes. So it was that when Christina and I drew apart suddenly and looked at one another, it didn't matter that I had pulled away, muttering an apology, as if an apology, at that moment, could be anything other than insulting.

'What do you mean?' she said. 'What are you sorry for? I'm not sorry . . .'

I stepped out of the circle our bodies had configured on the riverbank and turned my head away. 'I didn't intend for this to happen,' I said. 'It's wrong – '

'What do you mean, wrong?' She was angry now and I thought for a moment that she was going to hit me. 'Look at me!' I turned my head to face her. 'Don't you tell me – '

She got that far, before I interrupted.

'I didn't think,' I said quickly. 'I wasn't thinking. I lost my head. I'm sorry.'

'It's all right,' she said, her voice softening. 'We both lost our heads. But it's not as if – '

I shook my head. 'No,' I said. 'It wasn't your fault. I made a mistake, that's all.' Then, before she could say anything else, I turned and started walking away. It was dark now, so it was hard to see the path and I could hear her behind me, following for a few paces, then stopping. I walked on. 'Wait,' she said. 'Don't just go . . .'

I wanted to go back, I wanted to erase that contact between us, to turn the clock back to the moment just before she caught up with me on the path and repeat to fade, but that was impossible. All I could do was get away. I thought she would follow, but she didn't, and she didn't speak again, other than to call out, just loud enough for me to hear, one word that I only just made out. The word: *Coward!*

Next day she was gone. No word of goodbye, no explanation – or not until Kristen told me, supposedly in confidence, that Christina had run off with Neil on a journey across England by hot-air balloon. 'Eddie's *crushed*,' she said. 'But it's his own fault, really.' She allowed herself a moment's pause to study my face, hoping for a signal, a response. I managed to remain only mildly curious. 'He had his chances, he just didn't take them,' she said, with a wry smile – and I knew that she wasn't really talking about Eddie.

I shook my head, just a little too deliberately. 'I don't think she was that interested in Eddie,' I said. 'He's probably better off.'

'Maybe.' She allowed herself a grim smile. 'What surprises me is that Neil didn't move in sooner. I mean, she's a pretty girl, in her own way, and you know what Neil is like.'

'Do I?'

She laughed brightly, a laugh that implied a hint of reminiscence and, possibly, of girlish regret, either one of which, to my mind, would have to have been feigned. 'Neil is Neil,' she said. 'The poor girl won't know what hit her.' She went back to studying my face, and I went back to seeming impassive. 'That boy is a heartbreaker,' she continued, a touch too deliberately. 'And, as we all know . . .' she leaned in close for effect, 'he goes like a bunny.'

At any other time, I would have laughed; it was such a juvenile thing to say, but on this occasion, Kristen had chosen exactly the right phrase. It was ugly, vulgar, childish, but the image it conjured up made me feel as if I'd just swallowed vinegar. I had put so much effort into pushing Christina into running away, and now that she was gone, shagging her way across England with vacuous, pretty-boy-rich-kid Neil, I felt desperately, hopelessly lost.

It was the most exquisite sensation.

SIXTH DIGRESSION: WHY BEING LOST
IS AN INSTANCE OF GOOD FORTUNE

Quite early one May morning, in the last days of a subarctic winter, I strayed from a marked trail I had been walking for just under two hours and discovered that I was lost in the north Norwegian tundra. It was something that never should have happened: ninety-nine times out of a hundred, I am a sensible, even cautious wanderer, but that morning, in an odd mood I couldn't explain other than to say, lamely, that I was sorry to be leaving Finnmark, I had left the borrowed lakeside cabin where I'd been staying and decided to go for one last walk along a not at all hazardous eight-mile trail about thirty miles east of Kautokeino. I had all the right gear, or most of it – layers of thermal clothing, a good map, a pocketful of energy bars in case the walk took longer than expected – but, really, this wasn't one of those serious, adventure-trail, orienteering-type walks. It was just a last wander to say a mental goodbye before driving my hire car back to Lakselv and taking the shuttle plane down to Tromsø to spend Grunnlovsdag (Norway's equivalent of Independence Day) with friends. I said goodbye to my host – an elderly woman with a broken leg, a friend of a friend of a friend who had agreed to let me use one of her holiday cabins for a week, though it was out of season and, as she said, 'the stove was cold' – and I didn't worry too much when, going over my things, I discovered I had lost my compass. I didn't even bother to check the forecast. I just headed out. I'd had a fine time in the area around Kautokeino, walking each day on set trails over empty tundra or along the river, the last snow still glittering in the sun at midday and not dirty yet, though the night skies were already white, a thin, grey twilight settling over my little lake in the wee hours and every sign that the big thaw was on the way. It was the thaw that I had come north to see or, rather, to hear: I'd been told about the odd sound that came when the snow finally loosened its grip on the Finnmarksvidda – a sweet, musical sound that, if you could be quiet and still for long enough, you might sometimes hear quite clearly – and, though it may seem eccentric to travel thousands of miles to hear snow melting, this sound was the real, if secret, reason for my journey. By then, I had been to the north several times and I knew that, here, what begins as silence is really a nuanced fabric of faint or far-off murmuring: inhuman voices on the wind; the distant, soft pulse of something unidentifiable coming through a stand of birch woods near Karasjoka; the cries of a drowned girl from centuries ago calling through the moans and rumblings of the Alta River at Pikefossen. This time, I was hoping to stand out on the high plain and listen to that thaw-water music, but the hard cold had returned unexpectedly and, less than halfway through my walk, it started to snow, slowly at first and then, quite suddenly, in thick, quick gouts, so when I finally realised I'd somehow strayed off the trail – that I had, in fact, probably left it some time ago – I couldn't follow my footprints back to safer ground. For several minutes, the idea that I was lost was so absurd I didn't quite believe it. Even when the knowledge sank in, I experienced just the briefest sensation of panic, and not for any sensible reason, but because I was supposed to be returning my car the next morning, and if I didn't get back and call home, my wife would fret. After that, I became quite calm and, though I am all too aware of how odd this sounds, I have to confess I felt something close to happiness. I was *lost* – though surely not very lost – on the high tundra, with snow falling around me and visibility about half what it was when I set out, and I was happy. It was only hours later, when I found myself sitting in the car, numb with cold and aching with fatigue, that I realised how scared I should have been. At the time, however, my first recognisable emotion was a quiet sense of actually being in the world, a thread of its fabric, stupid and vulnerable perhaps, but alive and more alert than I had been in a long time. Certainly, I felt more real than I ever felt at home. I was a lost creature, happily coming to his senses, even though I was in a place that I didn't understand in the least and into which I might, quite literally, disappear. That exhilaration didn't last, of course, and it really was a matter of luck that I eventually got out of there.

To say that I should have known better than to go wandering off into the snow of the high *vidda* is a serious understatement. By the time of my Finnmark misadventure, I had been travelling to the Arctic Circle for several years and should have been more respectful of the terrain My first visit in 1996 was to a conference in Tromsø, and, for reasons that I couldn't explain at the time – reasons that had more to do with déjà vu than conscious choice – I'd felt compelled to return ever since, usually once, sometimes twice a year. I am not sure I can adequately relate how strong this sense of being suddenly and uniquely at home in the far north was; what I *can* describe is the memory of that first arrival, a memory of slowly descending out of a high white sky towards a landscape that looked and felt immediately as if I had secretly belonged there all my life – a place that, had I not known how far I was from my own house, I would happily have called home. That sense was utter and immediate and I will never forget how intense it was.

Of course, I had thought and spoken of other places as 'home', and I had meant it, in the casual way we mean the things we've been taught, but as this northern island rose to meet the plane in its descent, I knew that, with each of those homes, I had settled too easily for an illusion. It goes without saying that I am all too aware how ready I am to shift the furniture of recollection around for convenience or dramatic effect, but this sense of finding home wasn't a realisation that I came to in the course of time. It was immediate and true, and so close to overwhelming that, when the plane touched down and the other passengers disembarked, I had to stay in my seat for a while, gathering myself. What I had felt, on that descent, was an extraordinary sensation, as unsettling as it was pleasurable and, as I finally emerged from the plane, under the watchful eyes of a concerned flight attendant, I couldn't help feeling that I was betraying something, or someone, in the life I had just left behind – a life that suddenly felt like backstory.

That dual sensation – of finding and, at the same time, betraying home – only grew stronger with time. For my second trip, I went to Rovaniemi in northern Finland, and walked out in the bright, crisp white of the January snows to stare at an astonishing, powder-blue shaman's mask at the Arktikum Centre, but more often than not I headed for Tromsø, to stay with a philosopher I'd met at the 1996 conference and with whom I had become instant friends – and, again, there had been an element of déjà vu in this, like meeting a brother, even a twin, I didn't know I had. A native of the southern region of Telemark, my friend had come north as a young man and it may be that he saw in me the same fatal attraction to the north that he had experienced. He had also caught sight of something else in me, something dangerous. One day (it was early September and the last day of my visit), we were on one of our rambles around the lesser islands of the archipelago along the Troms coast: Kvaløya, where I dreamed of living in the lonely, grey-blue wooden house I had seen on the shore road near Mjelde, then Sommarøya with its white beaches littered with ghostly cold-water corals, and, finally, on the westernmost tip, the rocky last stand of Hillesøy. It was rather a fine day, some-what past summer's end, and though I would have been content to sit talking in his kitchen, as we usually did on the eve of my departure, I think the reason he drove me out there was to warn me, in his understated way, about what he'd seen. As it happened, that warning didn't register till much later, and maybe it only started to sink in when I finally abandoned my dreams of living in the far north and settled into the inevitability of here – the place where I work, where my children go to school and where, undoubtedly, I am doomed to belong.

I wouldn't want to make too much of this. My friend is

unobtrusive and tactful, and I don't want to suggest that he
was preaching, or pulling me up, on that day's walk around the
outer islands, culminating, as always, at the far end of Hillesøy,
a place I had christened 'the end of the world'. Of course, to
the child in us, almost everywhere has its world's end, but
Hillesøy's is more convincing than most. It's not picturesque,
just a series of wooden houses painted in various shades of earth
red and powder blue and ochre, terminating in a battered,
wind-bleached boathouse and, just beyond it, a path that leads
out to low cliffs over a dark, almost midnight-blue sea. The
vegetation is scrubby and brittle at summer's end, but it's never
very startling: the Arctic Circle contents itself, mostly, with
minor miracles, the subtle shades of mauve and orange lichens,
an immense range of greys and fogged blues and, in the right
season, the stark beauty of the Arctic poppy, a slender grey-green
plant with pale-yellow, near-translucent flowers that turn
constantly to face the sun through its daylong journey around
the summer sky. Elsewhere, there are gentians and tiny saxifrages,
too small to see until the eye learns this northern light well
enough to pick them out among the blown grasses and the
moss. In early September, the only colour was the occasional
orange-yellow bauble of a cloudberry amid the dry ling, and
the not quite pea green of the *kråkebolle*, those little sea urchins
that gulls snatch from rock pools and carry high into the air,
soaring above the cliffs and then letting the little bodies fall
over and over again till they break on the rocks below and the
tangle of edible ooze and viscera hidden within the shell is
exposed. My favourite thing to do on Hillesøy is to walk out
to the edge of the land and fix my eyes on the horizon – and

that was what I did, while my friend trailed behind discreetly, allowing me a moment of the solitude he had come out here to savour so many times himself. There are places where we can make out the curvature of the earth and I always think I can see it out there – and it is always pleasing, for reasons that I don't fully understand. All I know is that it has more to do with proportion than with size or significance. After a long moment, my friend caught me up. He had found a good cloudberry, which he offered to me as a token of hospitality, me being the visitor. 'Taste it,' he said.

I knew this wasn't the best place for cloudberries, but this particular specimen was fat and juicy – though not sweet. Cloudberries are never sweet. They aren't supposed to be. 'It's very good,' I said; then I turned and looked back out across the dark water. I was happy, as I always was when I came to the world's edge, but I had no idea why. In front of me there was a stretch of dark blue water; behind me, a rugged, but not particularly imposing or picturesque headland. It wasn't special in any way, certainly not guidebook material. We had stopped talking now, but I was quietly aware of a shared sense of the place and the moment that is the bedrock of companionship – and it did seem to me, then, that we were there for the same reasons. It was an assumption I had always made; like me, my friend surely loved the north because here, out on these lonely islands, he could find the isolation that his mind and his soul needed. But that assumption was mistaken, in small yet significant ways, and that day, after a long, mostly silent drive back along the coast road that skirts the deep, elk-haunted woods of the interior, I began to see how much I was taking for granted.

All the way home, I knew something was on his mind, but my friend is one of those rare men who weighs up everything he says and it wasn't until we reached the outskirts of the city that he began to speak. Even then, he didn't really say that much and his voice was innocent of any accusation or irony; still, his intention was clear, even if I didn't make out the full burden of his words till later.

'This is a special place for you,' he began, quite conversationally, as we passed the stores at Kvaløysletta.

I nodded. 'More than anywhere else, I feel completely at home on Kvaløya,' I said, though I was aware I was only repeating what he already knew.

He nodded in turn. 'Yes,' he said. 'And if you could, you would buy that little blue house at Mjelde and spend the rest of your life there, wouldn't you?'

'Yes,' I said.

'Perhaps you would be happy there. Alone, quiet, able to work. You'd be right at home.' He had his eyes fixed straight ahead, now that we were in traffic. 'But there is something you should consider.'

I laughed awkwardly. 'I wouldn't worry about it,' I said. 'It's not going to happen – '

'Maybe not,' he said. 'But you have to remember, just in case, that you don't come north to get away from people.' He shot me a brief glance, but I didn't say anything, and he turned back to the road. The firmness in his voice had taken me by surprise. 'It's not about romantic isolation, no matter how attractive that might seem,' he said. 'In fact, it's quite the opposite.'

For a moment, then, I allowed myself to imagine that I didn't know why he was telling me this. I had never made a big, Garboesque production of wanting to be alone, or not that I had noticed, though of course the truth was that I understood immediately. I am one of those people who dreams of having not just a moment's quiet, or a chance to work, but a solitary existence, and some of the choices I have made in my life, choices that I do not regret but don't wholly understand, continue to surprise me. Choices that involve being with others. Choices that involve me doing exactly what I say I have no desire to do, in places I have no desire to be. 'Up here,' my friend continued, not looking at me, 'you have to get along with people. Not just individuals, but everybody. Avoiding them isn't really an option because at any moment you might need your neighbour in order to survive. And that's any one of your neighbours – you can't pick and choose.' He let out a soft laugh and shook his head. 'I don't say that people here are any better than they are elsewhere. But, given the circumstances, they have to be able to trust each other.' He turned then, and looked me in the eye – and I immediately saw that he was talking about himself as much as me, about the younger self he had been when he moved north. 'It's not what you think,' he said. 'Really. You can't live here in splendid isolation. You may think you want that, but you don't. You'd go mad in the end, believe me.' He turned back to the traffic. 'Here, it's not about solitude, it's about having a real community. Once you have community, then you can be alone. That sounds like a paradox, but it isn't really. When you go out to the edge of the world, you have to have something to come back to. You may not come back very often, but you have to know that you can. Otherwise, you're lost.' He gave another little shake of the head, and I could see that he was being a little theatrical, to take the edge off the lesson he was giving me. 'To be alone, you have to know there's a real community you can trust.' He nodded slightly, confirming something – for himself, I thought, more than for me. 'Without that, you're not really alone at all,' he said. 'You're just – hiding.'

Had I been honest that day, I could have admitted that the idea of community had always been a problem for me, but not because I wanted to be alone, Garbo-style, as my friend had suggested. On the contrary: for a long time I wanted to find a community to which I might honourably belong, but the kind of life I dreamed about was unavailable. Sure, there's always been fine rhetoric from politicos about 'community values', but what they're talking about is a continuation of the old inequal- ities, the hierarchy where everyone knew his place and the same people always ended up at the top, planning, guiding, benevolent dictators (in their own eyes, anyway) and self-appointed worthies. That kind of community isn't about equality and mutual support, it's about grace and favour and singling out the deserving poor – and that was more of a disappointment to me than I was prepared to admit. Growing up at the end of the 1960s, I had hoped, naively and very briefly, that my generation, having 'cleansed the doors of perception', would create a new order based on social justice and the seemingly limitless powers of the imagination. Then the backlash had come – and it had been not only brutal but also condescending. Vance Packard's analysis is typical: 'The rather desperate efforts of . . . hippies . . . to establish "tribes", farm "communities", and even communal pads might be viewed as an outspoken symptom of a more widespread yearning for "community".' I was never a hippie and I had never wanted to go back to some notion of a tribal or agricultural past, but for me, 'community' was a revolutionary idea, one that meant the most rigorous standards for societal relations. Justice. Inclusion. Equality. Respect, and an equal voice, for the freaks and the *thrawn*. I had been naive, no doubt about that, but I was never guilty of nostalgia. Eventually, however, it began to appear that a just, egalitarian community was a pipe dream and, like many of my contemporaries, I gave up on social engagement altogether. Now all that remained was the consolation of ecology, which in my case took the form of an idea of north and a sense that, somewhere in what eco-critics call 'the more than human', the natural order continued, whole and just and intact. To honour that inherent order, some of us adopted a proud and sterile form of internal exile, of being at least self-aware in what David Riesman calls 'the lonely crowd'. Yet while it may be true that there is some honour in refusing the false community on offer, if only for the sake of what Riesman calls the 'other figures in the landscape – nature itself, the cosmos', possibly even a deity of some kind, there is also the problem for the self-exiled of not being perfect. Marooned in the lonely crowd, the solitary has to be impeccable and without societal needs: to want anything is a sin that must never be confessed, in case the frustrated desire to belong is made public – and so comes to seem like a readiness to make dishonourable compromises. This is why turning away is as much a matter of grief as it is of honour, and the only thing that can assuage that grief, in the absence of a just belonging, is to vanish completely into the larger world.

197

To vanish completely. Perhaps this was my fantasy; but I knew I wasn't alone, for I had frequently chanced on the same fantasy in others. If there is one constant in late-nineteenth-century Norwegian art, it is the recurring play between appearing and vanishing, between remaining in this world and receding into another. We find it in Munch, of course (where being in this world can end in the horror of *The Scream*, with nightfall coming and the given world swirling and dissolving around you), but it is also present in the work of many other artists too: in Frits Thaulow, in Eilif Peterssen, in Kitty L. Kielland and, perhaps most notably, in the hugely underappreciated Harald Sohlberg, a painter at least the equal of Munch, but now barely known outside Norway. As it happens, I first came across Sohlberg in the Kunstmuseum in Tromsø, where a little painting of his captivated me at first glance. According to the museum guide, its title could not be translated into English, or not by a single term, but meant something like 'snow's loosening' or 'snow's melting', and it is astonishing how utterly Sohlberg captures that moment when, after four or five months of deep winter, the snow finally lets loose its grip on the land, and everything that had been so thoroughly buried – all the shapes, the colours, the textures – begins to emerge. It was a theme this painter returned to again and again, most notably in his great paintings of the Lillegaten in the town of Røros, where the blood reds and the pale, lit golds of the houses seem to have been renewed by their long absence throughout a Norwegian winter; or in *Fra Sagene* of 1911, with its astonishing greys and greens and subtle washed ochres, emerging from, or vanishing into, the snow and the gloaming. It's not clear which, but this is not important: what's important here, as it is in the winter paintings Sohlberg produced throughout his career, is the constant play between coming and going, between the vanishing and the re-emerging that consumes and renews the things of this world. In these works, the colours are both vivid and almost unbearably transient, yet there is nothing else I can think of in Western art that so wholly captures the play of reality, a play that undermines our sense that the world consists of solid facts and material things. This great painter never quite shed the suspicion that even his admirers didn't understand him: 'It is probably true,' he said, 'that for simple and naive reasons my works have aroused sympathy. But I maintain that they have by no means been properly understood for the pictorial and spiritual values on which I have been working consistently over the years.' By the time he died, in 1935, he had withdrawn from the world so utterly that one obituary described him as a forgotten man and expressed a hope that the 'coldness with which he surrounded a name that had been famous in his day, would now thaw'. And yet, while there is no doubt that Sohlberg saw his retreat as a necessary act – he believed wholeheartedly in the idea of the solitary and mostly misunderstood genius – the final irony of his decision is that much of the later work is considerably less interesting and quite often descends into self-caricature, or chocolate-box picturesque. But then, maybe the painting wasn't what mattered any more. Maybe it was the solitude. The being alone; the striving to be impeccable. Maybe that was the real work of art. I didn't vanish into the snow on that last walk in Finnmark, but it took me a long time to find the way back to the car, and when I did, it was through no virtue or skill of my own. As far as I can work it out now, I wandered in circles for hours and then, because the snow had abated and because by some fluke I chanced on something I'd seen before – almost a miracle in itself, in that constantly shifting terrain – I managed to work out where I was in relation to the last trail marker I had seen. What I had chanced on should have been more transient than anything else on that day of ever-shifting weather – it was a sort of hollow, almost like a small cave, in the frozen snow that had accumulated over a stream – and must have altered in the several hours that I had been wandering, but it was recognisable enough that I remembered it. Of course, when I eventually found the first trail marker, I still didn't know the shortest route back to the road (nothing, at this point, looked familiar at all). Eventually, after a walk that must have lasted around twelve hours, six or seven of them lost, I saw the car, a strangely alien-seeming sky-blue metal object that looked far too small for any real purpose. It was night now, and if it had been any earlier in the year, I might never have seen the car. I had been ridiculously lucky; but it was only when I got in and turned on the heating that I really understood just how much. I'd been hopelessly ill-equipped for getting lost on the tundra: I had gone out without a compass, I had no idea how to read a map in a place where there were no obvious landmarks and, most significantly of all, nobody had known I was there. There was no community behind me, there was just me – and, but for the grace of something or other, I might have vanished forever. But then, hadn't I known that all along? Had this not, in fact, been the entire point of the exercise? The thought crossed my mind,

I admit, but as I started the engine and pulled away, my head throbbing now and my hands numb on the wheel, it wasn't something that I wanted to pursue – not with so many more hours of driving ahead, and a longer road still to go before I would make it home.

HUMOR ME

(*Pere Ubu, 1977*)

By the time Christina returned from her ballooning adventure, late in the summer, I had already drifted away from her friends, so I didn't know she was back in town. I'd started on my new job – a real job, more or less, teaching General Studies at my alma mater to block-release vocational students, after the previous incumbent had a breakdown. The college adjoined a graveyard and, very soon, between talking aesthetics with first-year caterers and discussing the psychology of humour with a classroom full of profoundly humourless brickies, I got into the habit of wandering among the headstones, reading the names of the dead, who were more companionable, to my mind, than the living. I'd never been convinced by the idea of a hereafter, sweet or otherwise, but I didn't think of these lunchtime companions as altogether absent either. I once had a girlfriend who believed she could remember her former lives – not the whole narrative, just images and fleeting moments, like the tattered memories of a film seen long ago and now mostly forgotten – and she thought we all came back, reincarnated over and over again, paying off karmic debts and fulfilling broken promises in an eternal circle of birth and decay. To her mind, mortality was how we shared the world – with others, and with the wiser and more graceful versions of ourselves that were still to come. I reconsidered that notion quite often as I walked from headstone to headstone, or sat by the grave of a particularly attractive-sounding departee – an Elizabeth, say, or a Sarah Jane – eating the lunch I had bought from Arjuna, on Mill Road. I didn't actually believe any of it was true, but it's not necessary to believe an idea to find it elegant.

Why Christina was in the cemetery that day I will never know. Maybe she saw me crossing Mill Road outside the whole-food store and followed me down to the peaceful corner I had picked out for my simple picnic lunch of dried figs and banana loaf. This was my regime now: no drugs; simple food; whenever possible, solitude. Everything had changed: after the caravan and the shared house on Mill Road, I had taken a room in Newnham, on the top floor of a house that belonged to an elderly ex-journalist, the sister of a friend of a friend. The woman was rarely at home, however; she had a flat in London, and visited Cambridge only occasionally. I was, in a sense, more caretaker than lodger, though my duties were light (to date, all I had done was mow the lawn) and the rent was low. Also, the house was both convenient for Grantchester Meadows and a pleasant half-hour walk from the college.

'It's nice when somebody tells you about their uncle,' Holden Caulfield says, in *The Catcher in the Rye*. 'Especially when they start out telling you about their father's farm and then all of a sudden get more interested in their uncle. I mean it's dirty to keep yelling "Digression!" at him when he's all nice and excited. I don't know. It's hard to explain.' There are other reasons, however, for drifting away from the story one is trying to tell. In this case, I digress because I don't want to set down *in so many words* what passed between Christina and me that day. No doubt she *had* seen me by chance and followed me to the graveyard, and I am guessing that she was unsure of what she would say when she caught up with me. Maybe she wanted to explain that she hadn't gone off with Neil – or not in the way I had assumed; maybe she just wanted to repeat what she had said that last night, when I left her on the Meadows: to say it again, straight to my face, knowing, not only that she was right, but that I knew it. When she saw me take my usual seat in the graveyard and look back along the path to see her standing there, she might have been disarmed by the setting, or by the changes she must have seen in my face, now that she was close enough to notice. Because I *had* changed: I was already starting to become a different person – and losing her had played a significant part in that change. There were things I had given up because I had given her up, things I had convinced myself it was good to be without. I was lighter, sparer and, had I but known it, ripe for the madhouse. Maybe, for a moment, she even thought she had mistaken me for someone else: the twin I had lost at birth, perhaps, come down from the moon to take my place, because when she spoke, her voice betrayed a note of uncertainty. 'John?' she said. 'It *is* you . . .'

I stood up. 'You're back,' I said, trying to seem casual. 'When did you . . .?'

She shook her head. 'I'm not, really. I mean . . . I'm just about to . . .' She looked away, back to where the living were going about their business. 'My flight leaves on Friday.'

I nodded. Was I sorry? Relieved? I didn't know. I had given her up, but that didn't mean I could have gone on living in the same city as her, knowing that she was there. 'I imagine you'll be glad to get home,' I said. 'You've been away a long time.'

She shook her head again, then she stepped past me and sat down on the bench. I was making small talk, I knew, and I also knew she hated that. I sat down too, still clutching my lunch bag. Had I put it down, and reached out, I could have touched her. She gave me a sidelong look. 'Why did you run away?' she said, with no trace of emotion or hurt in her voice, as if she were simply curious for an explanation. 'All that time, why didn't you say anything?' She sat very still, studying my face.

I looked off to the side, where a Victorian couple and several of their children were buried. Had they been in love, the day they married? Had he been kind to her? Had she secretly loved someone else, someone who wasn't suitable, or was bound by duty to another? I took a breath, then turned to face her. 'What was I supposed to say?' I asked.

'It wasn't the *what* that mattered,' she said. 'It wasn't *the words*. All you had to do was say something. Anything. I would have understood.' She sat very still, watching me, waiting for some kind of response – only I couldn't think what to say. I had been angry with her for going off with Neil, even after I'd learned that they weren't lovers at all and that Kristen had been lying. My confidante had been another member of the inner circle, an American art student called Stella who, for some reason, had taken a liking to me and, though she had known Kristen since schooldays, didn't approve of her meddling in other people's lives. 'All you had to do was speak,' Christina said again. 'You knew I wanted you to. And I know you wanted me.' She sat quiet again, watching me, waiting for a response. When it didn't come, she shrugged and looked away. 'Or are you saying you didn't?'

There was hurt in her voice now – and if I *had* been less of a coward, I could have said something, but I didn't. I couldn't tell her that I didn't want her, because I wanted her desperately; and I couldn't tell her that this was the very reason I had refused her. I didn't understand why, not then, and not now, after over thirty years of asking myself the question; all I can say is that the sensation was somewhat like the moment in Natsume Soseki's[32] novel *Kokoro*, in which a young man speaks of his 'instinctive yearning' for women, then goes on to qualify that remark with the words: 'But the yearning in me was little more than a vague dream, hardly different from the yearning in one's heart when one sees a lovely cloud in the spring sky. Often, when I found myself face to face with a woman, my longing would suddenly disappear. Instead of being drawn to the woman, I would feel a kind of repulsion.' When I first read this, I was a little distracted by the quaint language, but I recognised the sensation; or rather, I recognised something like it, a perverse satisfaction in having refused what I most desired, not so much out of repulsion as a sudden detachment, or dissociation, a

---

[32] 'It is painfully easy to define human beings. They are beings who, for no good reason at all, create their own unnecessary suffering.' (Natsume Soseki: *I Am a Cat*)

remoteness from my own wishes that I could not explain and wouldn't have predicted. That day, as Christina waited for me to speak, the remoteness kicked in again and I felt a kind of blissful indifference, even though she was so beautiful to me, so desirable, that I could scarcely bear it. I had been in love with her from the first, in love, longing, and yes, yearning for her in that old-fashioned *Kokoro* manner since the night we'd met in Kristen's kitchen – but as soon as she let me know, in so many words, that she returned that love, I froze. Yet even I can admit that this is only part of the explanation – and the key to something like the full story is that word 'yearning'. Reading that passage, I immediately decided that 'yearning' was wrong. It was just too quaintly romantic, and I quickly transmuted it into 'desire'. But the point is that what the young man in the novel feels, and what I felt when I was with Christina, cannot be passed off as desire, because it is more powerful than wanting. It is a threat to the self, a descent into *amour fou* and, at the same time, a violent affirmation of the underlying, *thrawn* logic that our workaday logic tries so desperately to conceal.

When she spoke again, Christina's voice was touched with something like disgust, disgust or maybe contempt. 'Are you just going to sit there and say nothing?' she said. 'Can't you even do me the – ' She stood up. 'I love you,' she said. 'And I know you love me.' Her voice softened. 'All you have to do is say so, and I will do anything you want.'

I stood up too, still clutching my bag of food. It felt crumpled and greasy in my hand. 'I have to go,' I said. 'I'm teaching a class – '

'What did you say?'

'I'm teaching at the college now,' I said. 'I have a class at two . . .'

'Are you serious?'

'We can meet later,' I said quickly. 'We can talk – '

'We *are* talking,' she said. 'Now.'

'I have a class,' I said. 'I'll meet you later – '

She shook her head. 'No you won't,' she said.

'I will,' I said. 'Five o'clock. On Parker's Piece.'

A long moment passed. She didn't believe me, but it didn't matter now. She was tired. There had been enough cowardice, enough humiliation. 'You really are a coward,' she said quietly. She gave a thin sigh and shook her head slightly. 'All right,' she said. 'Five o'clock. Where the paths cross.'

'I'll see you there,' I said.

She nodded, but she didn't say anything more. She just turned and walked back towards Mill Road slowly, like somebody out for an afternoon stroll. I don't know if she knew I wasn't going to show. She probably did, though I imagine she went anyhow, just to be sure.

I never saw Christina again. When she got back to Minnesota she sent me an angry, yet strangely touching letter that would have shamed me, had I been any closer to myself than I was in those days. But I was far away, cold and hollow, utterly dulled by the past several years of alcohol and drugs and emotionally extenuated. The only other item in the post that day was a chain letter and, in an act of childish cruelty, I forwarded it to her the next morning. I felt whittled out, empty, but also clean, as if I had come in from a long run and stood a long time in a cold shower: it was such a physical event, this sad, local betrayal that I had committed in exchange for – what? To be alone again? To stop having to think about her all the time? If I believed that, I was sorely mistaken. I made no other attempt to reply to her, and when she wrote me one last time, to say how hurtful it had been to go to the mailbox and find *that* envelope addressed in my hand, I tossed that letter in a waste bin on the way to work. I thought it would be easy to forget what I had done – and maybe it would have been, if I had felt even a little ashamed of myself at the time. But I didn't feel anything. I put it all to the back of my mind, where it grew and flourished, like mildew.

In fact, the shame didn't come until much later. Shame and disgust, but also a genuine bewilderment as to why I had acted as I did, and it was the bewilderment that, over the course of several weeks, became close to unbearable – until, eventually, I learned how to romanticise it all, to make it a story that consigned us both, Christina and myself, to a dream life whose effect, in the end, was very much like a death. Somehow, we had parted, as death might have parted us, but we had loved one another and it wasn't certain that we'd never meet again. That was a fantasy I sincerely entertained: I would be walking on a street in London or New York – somewhere, anywhere, though never Cambridge – and we would meet by chance, older and wiser and ready to take up where we had left off. I didn't know that this was a sign of grief; how could it be, when I'd had nothing taken from me, when I was the one who had thrown it all away?

But there was something else going on here too. Now that she was gone, Christina became my most intimate secret. I never talked about her, because she wasn't part of my daily life, she existed in the past and in the future, and I was simply waiting for fate to do what fate does and bring us together again. I never talked about what had happened, not to anyone; that story just hung there, suspended in the cradle of my flesh, still as a tumour. There was nobody to josh me out of it all and tell me to grow up and stop being so stupid; there was no cynic to point out that I simply hadn't got to know Christina enough to tire of her – to discover her annoying habit of leaving the top off the cliché toothpaste tube, or her secret fondness for Loggins & Messina. I was quite sure that nobody I knew would understand the injury I had inflicted on us both, because I didn't understand it myself. Why had I refused her? Why had I behaved as I did? I couldn't find a good answer, not even in the pages of Japanese novels; so now that she was safely far away, I changed the script. I romanticised it all and so made it bearable – and yet, in spite of all this romanticising, in spite of the fact that I thought about her constantly, I never made any attempt to contact her, or to apologise for what I had done. I guarded my betrayal like some fascinating wound, secretly proud and horrified in equal measure. On the other hand, I have to accept the possibility that I rejected Christina for the very banal, workaday reason that I was afraid we might turn into a mere couple. Like my parents, say. Like everybody's parents. *I put a spell on you.* Annie had been right to mock it, because if you're *mine*, like the song and the marriage vows and the gaze of everyone around us says, then we can't play any more. The game is over. No play and, so, the end of the erotic. It wasn't just perversity to refuse that whole scenario of being together forever, it made sense in the most common of ways to say: If I want this, not as I want other things, but completely and for a lifetime, then it has to be refused. Walk away. Move on in your own head. Go. Or sit inert, like a stone, while the person you love tries to shake you back to life. There's a perverse satisfaction in that stillness, that obduracy, but it doesn't last. Four days after Christina's second letter, I woke up on a stranger's floor in a part of town that seemed much rainier than usual. I was in a two-bedroom flat with old-fashioned sash windows and almost no furniture. All the doors were open bar one, which I surmised led to the main bedroom and I could feel that someone was in there, sleeping. For some time, thinking it would be the more courteous gesture to do so, I stood waiting, gazing out of the window (it seemed that the flat was on the second floor of a terraced house), at the wet gardens and the grey, empty streets, but nobody appeared from the bedroom, and eventually I got bored and, having let myself out quietly, walked home in the rain. I never did find out whose flat that was or how I had come to be there.

SEVENTH DIGRESSION: ON THE MOUNTAINS OF THE MOON

Eighteen months after I last saw Christina – eighteen months, which is clearly too long a time for there to be a connection, or so I choose to maintain – I was admitted to Fulbourn Mental Hospital, a leafy and surprisingly pleasant institution three or four miles outside Cambridge. I don't remember very much about the week or so that led up to this point, but I heard later that I had been hallucinating for several days and I still recall images and fragments from what may well have been a meaningful, if decidedly bizarre, narrative, a story I was telling myself in a last-ditch attempt to create order in a life that had, by that stage, become hopelessly chaotic. What others knew about these hallucinations I never fully established – did I talk about them? Was I even capable of descriptive speech? – and my own memories are patchy, to say the least. At one point, a series of tiny ballerinas pirouetted across a linoleum floor; then, several hours or possibly days later, a sleek, oddly beautiful creature, half-girl, half-swordblade, came into the room where I had been sleeping and sat quietly at the edge of my bed, her face kindly, her eyes fixed on mine. Not long after *that*, a man in a pearl-white suit emerged from the far end of a long corridor and, smiling all the while, as if this were some kind of blessing, shot me in the forehead with a bolt gun similar to the weapons that slaughtermen use on cattle. To this day, I feel sure that those memories are fragments and threads of a much larger story, a story with its own logic and direction, but I cannot remember, now, what that logic consisted of, or where the story was going. Like a sleeper who wakes suddenly from an almost unbearably complex dream, all I have is a wholly unjustifiable conviction that all of this *meant something* and, to this day, I wish, as I wished then, that I knew what it was. It seems an important failure, now, that I never worked it out, just as it seems irrelevant, looking back over my medical records, to discover that the official diagnosis of my mental state that summer was 'psychosis, of a paranoid nature'.

At that time, the routine treatment for psychosis of a paranoid nature was antipsychotic drugs such as chlorpromazine (which, despite its efficacy, in my own case at least, has since fallen out of favour) and a regime of quiet and containment. So it was that, during the next several weeks, I was gradually led back to something approaching normality. Soon, I was able to follow the routines of the hospital: wake-up call; breakfast; medication; day room; lunch; medication; day room or a turn in the grounds; dinner; medication; day room; medication; sleep, with occasional patches of medication, if needed. This went on for quite some time, during which I was mostly oblivious to the other patients, and even to the staff, as I worked my way through the set timetable – oblivious, because I wasn't really present most of the time, and when I was, I became so absorbed in trying to work out how I'd got there that other people really did seem irrelevant.

Irrelevant is a useful word, I find, in attempting to describe mental aberration: the most obvious characteristic of the mentally ill is their utter disregard for what other people consider important or necessary, while their sense of what *does* matter – an image on the back of a cereal box, a real or imagined moment from some far-off summer's morning, a phrase from a radio broadcast that invades the mind like a virus and breeds there, till there's little room for anything else – is entirely mysterious to outsiders.

I don't know how long I inhabited that private world of mine, and I don't know how long I might have stayed there, if I hadn't met Cathy, but one day, while contemplating yet another bran-laced lunch in the refectory (all the food in psychiatric hospitals contained added bran, to counter one of the more unfortunate side effects of the medication), I suddenly felt that someone was beside me, sitting to my left, our shoulders almost, but not quite, touching. Nobody had been there a moment before – paranoid psychotics tend, generally, to dine alone – but now, when I turned ever so slightly to sneak a sideways glance at my companion, I saw that I had been joined by a woman with long, dusty-blonde hair, in a flower-patterned, possibly quilted housecoat or dressing gown. She wasn't looking at me (and it occurred to me, later, that she may well have had no intention of sitting down next to *me* at all), but she was aware of the fact that someone or something was there, not so much a person from the actual world as a co-conspirator, or perhaps a witness, from her own imagined realm – and what she did next was part of a drama that had nothing at all to do with me, a drama that was almost wholly internal.

What she did next, in fact, was the act of a psychiatric patient, a mentally ill individual, yet it was also a work of art, and I still think that its purpose was to create order, just as a work of art attempts to create, or at least to clear the way for, a similar order in the wider world. As she rose, I could tell that she was checking to see if I – or rather, the presence for whom I was a surrogate – was watching her; then, assured that this was the case, she began to spin around on near-tiptoe, like a dervish, her arms outstretched, her body suspended in what felt like its own force field, sweet and wild and inviolable, turning perfectly in the honeyed sunlight that, at that very moment, was streaming in through the refectory windows, picking her out like a spotlight and isolating her, as she danced her terrible, rapt solo. I had been marooned in my own small world until that dance began; now, I had no choice but to turn and look round, no choice but to bear witness to what was happening – and, at that moment, I was struck, through the sweet haze of bran and chlorpromazine and the suspicion that the whole thing might be a last, parting gift from the hallucinatory state I had occupied for what felt like months, I was *struck*, as I say, by the sheer beauty of the moment and, at the same time, by the thought that, in order to reach such a state of grace, this woman, whom I did not know, had been obliged to let herself become mad and, so, fundamentally indefensible. It was beautiful, that dance, but it was also an act of the darkest celebration, an almost unbearable tribute to whatever it was in the world that was crushing her. Then, after what seemed a long time, but probably wasn't at all (had it gone on, the professionals would doubtless have intervened), this interlude was over and the woman was gone, leaving only a vague impression of movement and wildness on the air. Looking around, I saw that the other patients – lost in their own dramas or bent to their soup bowls, intent on following the prescribed regime to the letter – hadn't noticed a thing, and the woman – Cathy – was nowhere to be seen.

I didn't see her again, in fact, for several days and, when I did, she looked so slight and pallid, such a ghost of a person, that I barely recognised her. On that occasion, and on the two or three that followed, she ignored me, and I began to wonder if I had imagined the whole thing. Then, almost a week after our first encounter, she found me in the day room and sat down alongside me, her face fixed on the television screen that I had been doing my best to ignore.

'What's your name?' she said; then, without waiting for a reply, she added quickly: 'My name's Cathy.'

I looked at her. She was vivid again, not a ghost, the pallor gone, her eyes bright. Had she seemed just a little less febrile, she could have passed in the outside world for vivacious. 'John,' I said, noticing how dull my voice sounded – and I wanted to say more, but I couldn't think of anything *to* say.

'John,' she repeated, smiling. She gave me a long, appraising look. 'So. What are you in for, John?'

This was a question I couldn't answer. I hadn't been told the official diagnosis, I still couldn't remember the days imme- diately preceding my admission, and on the few occasions when I had taken the time to notice the other inmates on the ward, I felt utterly unlike them. In fact, whenever I was alone, I felt extremely lucid. I knew something had happened to me, and I knew it was intrinsic to who I was, but I didn't believe I was 'mentally ill'. I didn't even think I was *mad.*

Though the word was never used, and it took me years to apply it to the condition that I have been managing all my life, I can see now that I was suffering from a spike in the usual apophenia: the extreme tendency to find elaborate patterns and significance in everything. Meanwhile, as I would quickly learn, Cathy was a 'schizophrenic'. Actually, she was a 'classic schizophrenic' and, at times, her condition was almost ploddingly textbook: she believed that she had been injured in an accident and that her spleen – apparently the home of the soul – had been removed; she heard messages from some lost cosmonaut coming through the TV in the day room; she wanted to escape the hospital, but she couldn't leave, because 'they' were holding her daughters hostage – etc., etc. In the days that followed, she told me all these stories and, for most of the time, I believed her. It was, in fact, a sign that I was still unwell when I continued to believe, just as it was a sign of my recovery when I became, first, sceptical, then incredulous. Now, she was watching me, waiting for an answer to her question. I shook my head. 'I don't know,' I said.

Cathy laughed. This seemed to be funniest thing she had heard in months. 'You're funny,' she said. 'I think you're funny. Do you know that?'

I smiled. 'How am I funny?' The words felt like balls of felt in my mouth.

She laughed again. 'People are only funny when they don't know they're funny,' she said quickly. 'You should know that.' She studied my face and I could see that she was checking, making sure I was genuinely funny and not just faking it. A moment later, satisfied – or so it seemed – she sat back in her chair and looked up at the TV again. The man on the screen, an actor in an American TV series, was talking very earnestly to a courtroom full of people. '*He's* not funny,' Cathy said. She turned back to me. '*You're* funny,' she said. 'I hope you remember this.' Then, in a millisecond, her face changed, and she turned slightly, her head tilted to one side. 'Listen!' she said.

I listened. I couldn't hear anything, other than TV and, in a far corner of the day room, a man called Paddy, fast asleep and snoring in his usual chair. 'What is it?' I said.

She didn't answer. She was listening hard, the way an animal listens for a predator, out in the open somewhere, hopelessly exposed.

'What?' I said again – and though I couldn't hear what *she* was hearing, I was listening with her, actively listening and, later, I understood that this was the moment when she recognised me as a fellow traveller. Because – how to say this? – I wasn't *not hearing* on purpose, as others did, because they doubted her, I was just *not* hearing. 'I don't hear it,' I said – and I heard the disappointment in my voice, because I felt, not that she was having auditory hallucinations, but that I was missing something.

At that, Cathy looked at me and, for one moment, a flicker of suspicion passed across her face. Then, just as suddenly as she had tensed up, she relaxed. She smiled at me, her eyes still searching – not for signs of danger, this time, but for reassurance. 'Nothing,' she said. 'Nothing at all.' She stood up and looked around the day room with a surprised and slightly dismayed expression, like Bette Davis in some old movie. 'Shall we go for a walk?' she said – and it was clear, from her tone, that refusal was not an option.

It doesn't sound like a very auspicious beginning, I suppose, yet over the next few days, Cathy and I became new best friends and, aside from the obvious fact that we were neither of us normal, the basis of that friendship seemed to be that we were both *listeners*. For a long time, this seemed significant, as if it really might be true that the world was divided into two groups: those who heard voices in the radiators and cisterns and those who heard nothing but water – and I think I knew, even then, that people like us were doomed to spend the rest of their lives on the alert, listening for those whispers and catcalls in the plumbing. Even if we 'get well', even if we go back to the normal world and learn to *pass*, we can never stop ourselves from pausing, halfway through the afternoon, or in the small hours, suspended over a sink or standing stock-still in some washroom or hallway, pausing to listen, to test the water, to verify the silence. Because, of course, to stop hearing doesn't necessarily mean that there is nothing to hear any more and, even as the confirmation of a provisional and approximate sanity arrives, the suspicion remains that one is always missing something.

At the same time, I have to confess that I was drawn to Cathy, attracted by a force that seemed to me both entirely natural and utterly mysterious. It was partly sexual, no doubt, and it was certainly romantic, both in the usual meaning of the word, and in the sense that the woman I was drawn to was a myth, as much a creature of my own imagination as she was flesh and blood. She was not conventionally beautiful. On bad days, she was grey, pallid, almost non-existent; but at other times, there was a quality to her presence that seemed almost unbearably glamorous – by which I mean, glamorous in the old sense, not like a catwalk model or a starlet, and not, God help us, like a celebrity, but in the sense that Walter Scott uses it, the sense of creating a spell, of *casting the glamour*. The sense, in other words, of a verb rather than a noun, an influence rather than a state. Not the calculated theatre of celebrity, but the accidental drama of someone who unwittingly illumines the world as she passes through, unaware of the magic, blind to her own charms. For a time, I imagined I was in love with her – and, as I got better, I plotted to take her with me when I got out, so we could start a new life together, the old one-day-at-a-time, hard-at-first-but-gradually-winning-through, *amor vincit omnia* trip.

That fantasy didn't last, of course; but, for a while, we met every day and, often, we were close to happy. We felt like kin to one another, fellow travellers in a country where nobody else spoke the language, sitting in the day room or wandering the grounds, talking about nothing and everything, telling stories, philosophising and, sometimes, laying claim to some vague right that *they* were denying us, the right to be who and what we were, as opposed to the normal citizens that society wanted us to be. Gradually, however, I began to think of that right as a pyrrhic victory and, as the drugs took effect, it wasn't long before I was well enough to know how sick Cathy actually was and, soon enough, this awareness began to show. One day, in the hospital gardens, we saw a squirrel running across a patch of open ground ahead, and we stopped to watch as it paused, sat upright, studied us with a critical eye, then hurried a few yards further, just to be safe, before sitting up again and turning back to check that we were still out of range. Cathy turned to me. 'I feel sorry for animals,' she said.

'Why?'

'Because – ' She thought for a moment. 'Because they don't know they are going to die. Not till it happens, anyway. They haven't got that exchange to look forward to.'

I shook my head. I didn't understand what she meant by 'exchange' and I wondered if I'd misheard something – and then I thought that this was just some morbid wordplay, one of those wilful reversals that usually marked a change in her condition, from more or less normal, to pretty much gone. She would do that from time to time, launching out on a fantasy, with me as a sounding board; it would feel like a game at first, a diversion from the tedium of the hospital day, but it would quickly darken – like Mercutio's Queen Mab speech in *Romeo and Juliet*, folk philosophy in its wildest form, the merely baroque shading into the painfully grotesque in a matter of moments. 'I don't understand,' I said; but she didn't hear. She was watching the squirrel, and the squirrel was watching her – and it seemed, for a moment, that something was passing between them, a communication, an exchange. Then the creature darted away, and the spell was broken.

Cathy looked back to me. Her face was empty now, no glamour, no light and, at the same time, no distraction. 'Remember when you're a kid,' she said. 'How you know someone is watching you all the time? Everything you do, somebody sees it? And they tell you that person is God, or maybe you just think it must be God, because who else would be watching? Only it's not God. It's you. There's this exact replica of you and it's wandering around on the moon, walking in the mountains, because the moon has mountains, did you know this?' She turned to me, waiting for an answer, and I nodded. I *had* heard a story like this before, but I didn't know where. 'So, it's wandering about in the mountains of the moon,' she continued. 'And all the time it's watching you and when you die it comes and takes your place, and then you're there, on the moon – ' She stopped suddenly, and I could see she was listening for something. She listened for a minute or so, then she came back to where we were and looked at me, studying my face to see if I had understood, or if I thought she was just mad, like the rest of them. To begin with, she didn't know which; then she decided. 'I read that in a book,' she said, after a long moment. 'It's a comfort, don't you think?'

I nodded. 'Yes,' I said – and I realised that I wasn't just humouring her. I really *did* agree. It *was* a comfort.

Cathy smiled. 'You'll be going soon,' she said – and I knew she was right about that too. When our moods coincided, we agreed about everything, but now we agreed for different reasons. She was still mad, and I was almost ready to go back – and, though it had been obvious from the beginning, I realised for the first time that I would be going alone.

A few nights later, we sneaked out and walked to the nearest pub. It was a low-ceilinged, slightly too countrified place, but it was also close to deserted, which meant that it suited our purposes exactly. All we wanted was a drink and a corner to sit in, a nook where we could pretend we were normal people out for a walk, or on a date, and not loony-bin day trippers with the obvious signs of medication and recent hallucinations ghosting across our faces like shadows in a field of barley. Cathy was at her brightest – to begin with, at least – and the landlord, a big, sleepy man with a contented, slightly proprietorial air about him, was sufficiently glamoured to pretend that he didn't know where we'd come from. After he served us, we sat down in the furthest corner of the room, suddenly awkward, not with the sane world in which we knew we were interlopers, but with one another and, for some time, we didn't speak. Then, when we did, the conversation was random and jagged, and it felt as if we were performing lines from a script, the script of normality, where people talked very carefully about nothing. It was painful, but we couldn't stop it. We were out for a drink, we had escaped – and we were, as we both knew, here to say our goodbyes.

Finally, the quiet was broken by the arrival of a party of young locals – it was obvious, right away, that they *were* locals, from this or another of the surrounding villages, a party of eight, or rather, of four couples, boys home for the summer holidays with their home-for-the-holidays girlfriends, all of them well dressed in a smart-casual way and all of them known to the landlord, who no doubt knew and occasionally had a drink with their parents and so could vouch for the fact that they were good people. I watched them arrive and settle around a table, calling out orders to the tall, faintly tousled boy who had gone to the bar, debating choices, asking about the food – and I was charmed, I admit, by the air they had of liking their own

lives, and by the open and apparently genuine pleasure they
took in one another, not just the one they were with, but
the entire company. They were too well off, of course, and they
already seemed distantly young to me, but I didn't mind that.
I even allowed myself a moment of sentimental appraisal of the
unexpected vision they presented and, suddenly aware of
the fact that, for too long, my own pleasures had been etched
with black and half a wish for destruction, I felt an absurd, but
forgivable, desire to be *like* them. A normal boy, with a normal,
and very pretty, girl, out with friends, in a place I had always
known: that notion seemed, for a moment, both wonderful
and preposterous. I turned to Cathy. I suppose I was expecting
to catch a reflection of this sentiment in her eyes; instead, what
I saw was loathing.

'What is it?' I said. The expression on her face frightened me.
I looked back to the new arrivals, who were completely oblivious
to everything outside their own charmed circle, then I glanced
at the landlord – and I saw that *he* had seen, or sensed, that
something was going on in our corner. He was dealing with
his customers, smiling and talking about beer with the tousled
boy, but he had sensed trouble and he was on red alert, at the
back of his mind. No doubt he thought he was presenting an
easy face to the world, but he wasn't about to fool a paranoid
psychotic of my stature. I picked up my glass and drained it,
then I touched Cathy's arm, very gently. I could feel the tension.
'Let's go,' I said.

To my relief, she stood up right away – and I thought, to
begin with, that the situation might just be manageable. If I
could get her outside without incident, all would be well;

perhaps we could go somewhere, maybe buy a bottle of something and sit out for a while and have our goodbye drink. It was warm, still, not yet dark. All around, the countryside was touched with the dusty gold of after-harvest, dry and kindly and faintly sweet, like some old English folk song, and, for one moment, I imagined we could just leave and be on our way – but Cathy had other ideas. At first, she was talking to me, when she said it, her voice thin, not much more than a whisper, so quiet I could barely make out what she was saying. 'Who chose them?' she said; then she said it again, a little louder. 'Who chose them?' Then her voice rose: she wasn't shouting, quite, but she was calling out, accusing, judging. 'Who chose them?' she said, again. 'Who chose them? Nobody. They chose themselves.'

I took hold of her arm then, and began steering her towards the nearest exit, while she called back, not to the party at the other table so much as to the world in general, the same words, over and over, pausing for a second or two to consider each time she spoke, as if she thought the question could be better framed with a little effort. The door was only a few feet away, and we could have made it, but when Cathy spoke again, some of the other party looked up and, when she repeated her question for the fifth or sixth time, she had everyone's attention, the beautiful young people, the landlord, the two or three locals at the far end of the bar, all of them turning to stare at her, some in bewilderment, some amused, others just beginning to understand that a judgement was being pronounced and duly making ready to be offended. Meanwhile, the landlord was on his way round the bar.

'All right now,' he was saying. 'I think it's time – '

I didn't hear the rest. I knew what he wanted, and I wanted the same thing, but now Cathy was waving her free arm and pointing around the room, bearing witness, going cuckoo while the young people watched, bemused and concerned and, in some cases at least, a little scared. Meanwhile, I was trying to guide Cathy towards the door, a foot at a time, while the landlord advanced and I had visions of a scuffle, of police uniforms and doctors and people screaming. I looked across and saw that one of the young people had stood up, a dark-haired, rather flat-nosed boy in a rugby shirt and, though he wasn't moving in our direction yet, he was getting ready to be useful.

And then, in a matter of seconds, everything changed. Cathy turned to the landlord and her gesticulating arm suddenly dropped to her side. 'It's all right,' she said, her voice soft and oddly plaintive. 'It's all right. Don't be sad. Nobody's doing anything.' She was talking quickly, the way she had done when we first met. 'Nobody's going to hurt you. It's all right.' At this, one of the young people burst out laughing, and she turned to see – and at exactly the same moment the landlord slipped past me and opened the door, his eyes fixed on my face, as if he thought that, by choosing to pretend that Cathy didn't exist, he could ensure that any burden remained mine and mine alone, a matter of man-to-man, my taking this nuisance away and letting him go about his business. I don't know if he understood that I was a mental patient too but, if he did, it didn't matter, because I was the one who'd brought this woman to his pub, and it was my obligation to take her out again. I didn't entirely agree with this position, but I understood it and, now that the door was open, and the fresh air seeping in, I did what was necessary and, with some difficulty, manoeuvred Cathy through the exit and out, into the cool of the evening. Once we were safely outside, the door banged shut behind us, and Cathy fell silent. We stood there for a long time, not looking at one another, as if waiting for something that had been inter-rupted to start over again, a ghost machinery whirring in our minds, all smoke and mirrors. What had just occurred was, of course, a minor but altogether decisive betrayal. I had stood against her with the big world, and in so doing, I had declared myself *hors d'asile*: almost well, and ready to do what was neces-sary to pass for sane. I was still holding her by the arm, but I knew I didn't need to any more. The tension was gone and, after a few minutes' silence, she turned to me, her face calm, as if nothing had happened. Her eyes were bright, feverish-looking, but the glamour was gone. Now, she was like a guilty child who knows it has done wrong, but doesn't want to acknowledge the transgression. 'Shall we go for a walk?' she said. 'It's a lovely night.'

The next day, we met as usual and went for a walk in the grounds, but it quickly became obvious that a gap had opened between us. A week earlier, we had been denizens of the same scary and privileged world; now, I was somewhere on the outside, like a visitor at the zoo, peering through the bars, caught out in a vain and rather wistful attempt at fellow feeling. A few days later, I left the hospital. The staff didn't think I was ready, but I couldn't wait. I gathered the things I had accumulated – some spare clothes and toiletries and half a dozen books that a friend had brought in – and I put them in a plastic bag that one of the nurses gave me; then, alone and already painfully remote from the people around me, I sat in the day room, waiting for Cathy to come, so I could say goodbye. I waited a long time, but she didn't show. Sometimes that happened: either she would come floating into the room and sit down next to me, launching straight into the conversation that we'd discontinued the day before, or she would stay on her own ward, a grey, faraway creature, barely present, gazing into space. In the past, whenever she'd drifted away to that ghost place, I had wanted to go to her bedside and find some way of bringing her back, like Janet in the old story, who has to seize Tam Lin, the beautiful youth held captive by the Queen of the Fairies, and pull him from his horse, as he rides in the demonic procession – to pull him from his horse and back to earth, then hold tight, as the Queen transforms him, by turns, into a snake, then into a lion, and, finally, into a naked, newborn creature that she must conceal from the fairies' gaze, if she wants to keep him. Though, of course, I wasn't allowed at Cathy's bedside – and I knew it wasn't the Queen of the Fairies that had beguiled her. It was something lodged in her deepest self, a wet, dark, sweet-bitter, slightly greeny and, in all probability, timeless wraith that longed to exist in its own right, to have its own, independent life, to swim or fly or just walk free, dark and perverse enough to glamour the world forever with its eerie light. I think, that morning, as I made ready to leave and go back to the outside world, I still believed in this glamouring spirit, which no doubt meant that I was not quite as sane as I was supposed to be, but it was reason enough – a wrong reason, but also a better one than anything else I could have come up with – for taking up my plastic bag and walking away. At the time, I told myself that our parting was temporary, but I understand now that I was already preparing for the possibility of never seeing Cathy again; and it was true, I never did, though I came back twice to visit, only to be turned away, either because she wouldn't see me, or because the staff had decided that it wasn't in her best interests to continue what they saw as an inappropriate relationship. If I am honest, I suspect that this was probably a relief and, though I didn't think so at the time, I have to confess that I lost sight of her after that. Once I was out in the world, I became so preoccupied with trying to pass that I allowed myself to believe that any further visits would only upset us both. So it was a long while before I heard, completely by accident, that she was dead. Apparently, she had been in and out of hospital a couple of times; then, as part of a new flurry of cost-cutting measures in the health service, she was released into the care of 'the community' – no need to say how ironic this term inevitably seems, to people like us – and, some time later, she killed herself. I have no clear idea of why, where or how, but I suppose, when the body was discovered, someone with the appropriate qualifications made a series of textbook pronouncements, and she was laid to rest, while the dank, wet slick of her soul changed places with its doppelgänger, and wandered away to the mountains of the moon.

INTERLUDE: PORTRAIT OF MEL LYMAN

(*Diane Arbus, 1966*)

It was supposed to be an easy assignment: go in, keep a straight face, snap a few pictures of a former Kweskin's Jug Band banjo player who has suddenly decided he is God, then get out of there. What could be less complicated? Diane had been doing freaks and crazies for years now, humanising them, bringing out their essential humanity and, at the same time, turning them into beautiful monsters, beyond pity, beyond horror, perfected for an instant and made miraculous by the camera. None of this was exploitative; you could see she cared about these people, not because they moved her to compassion, or pity, but because she wanted to be them – or at least, to touch their lives for a moment, to bear witness to their natural aristocracy. Later, if you went down to Times Square or Hubert's Dime Museum and Flea Circus, that vivid creature you had stared at in the photograph would be gone, replaced by some shambling old con man or a deformed teenager in a badly altered swimsuit. No point in saying one was real and the other was an illusion. As Michelangelo Antonioni once remarked, 'The reality in which we live is invisible, so we have to be satisfied with what we see.'

Of course, if she wanted to take it any further, if she wanted to probe, even to expose the self-appointed divinity, then fine. After all, who better to penetrate the mask of the World Saviour than Diane Arbus? That was how they thought about it back at *Esquire* and *Harper's Bazaar*, because they assumed that, when people put on masks, their purpose is *to deceive*. They think we go masked because we want to hide our true selves, or because we are pretending to be something we are not. Divine beings; totem animals; innocents; celebrities. Though Arbus knows this is too simple – she has learned that, sometimes, when there is nothing in the face that addresses us, when the stare is blank, coming from a place where the person observed is alone and utterly indifferent to what we see, or think we see, it is the true self that presents as mask. And sometimes, when a boy looms out of the hard light of day in a plastic Halloween face, he really is, for that one moment, a monster.

It was supposed to be an easy assignment and – who knows? – maybe it was. Nobody made a record of what Mel Lyman and Diane Arbus talked about, if they talked at all, during that photo shoot in the mostly black Fort Hill area of Boston, where Lyman lived with his 'Family'. A year or so earlier, he had been divinely appointed to calm the outraged folkies at the 1965 Newport Festival after Bob Dylan went electric, playing a thirty-odd-minute riff on the old hymn 'Rock of Ages' while Dylan walked off into history (Lyman said later that it was 'like what Christ had to do before mounting the cross, he said not my will but thine be done and then there was no cross, no death'). Now, he had decided that he wasn't just the head of his Family, he was also an extraterrestrial Avatar who had taken human form to work towards 'world salvation'.[33]

So it's intriguing to speculate about the conversation between Lyman and Arbus that day. Maybe the World Saviour shared some of his views on women: 'If a woman is really a woman, and not just an old girl, then everything she does is for her man and her only satisfaction is in making her man a greater man. She is his quiet conscience, she is his home, she is his inspiration and she is his living proof that his life, his labours, are worthwhile.' That would have hit home. Arbus had married young and, for several years, she and her husband, Allan, had worked together, mostly on fashion assignments. By 1966, however, they were living apart. Arbus was making her own photographs, while Allan kept the studio going, but he was frustrated, torn between the need to support his family and his long-held acting ambitions (he would later play Dr Sidney Freedman in the TV series *M*A*S*H*). A man like Lyman might have picked up on that background tension, he might have sensed guilt or conflict in Arbus, who was on this supposedly easy assignment for health reasons. She had always been fragile, but right then, through the winter of '65 and into '66, she was

[33] How this was to be achieved was never fully formulated, other than in song lyrics, along such lines as: 'I am going to burn down the world / I am going to tear down everything that cannot stand alone / I am going to turn ideals to shit / I am going to shove hope up your ass / I am going to reduce everything that stands to rubble / and then I am going to burn the rubble / and then I am going to scatter the ashes / and then maybe someone will be able to see something as it really is / Watch Out!' (Mel Lyman: 'Declaration of Creation', *c*.1966–7)

pretty low, weak in the spirit and all too vulnerable. Some of her friends thought she shouldn't be working at all. Maybe Lyman dug a little and then, sensing vulnerability, dug a little more. It's possible that some of the Family's womenfolk, three of the younger, prettier women, say, are there in the room, exemplars of real womanhood, as opposed to the old girl who sits fiddling with her camera. 'A woman who seeks to satisfy herself is the loneliest being in God's creation. A woman who seeks to surpass her man is only leaving herself behind. A man can only look ahead, he must have somewhere to look from. A woman can only look at her man . . .' Lyman could go on like that for hours, laying down the law, and certainly the Fort Hill women lived by it.

But then, nobody knows what he said to her, or she said to him. Maybe she just set up the shot and left. The resulting portrait is fairly ordinary (though Lyman's pose is rather odd and, to a *real* forward-looking man, he might have come over as a little effete). On the other hand, it takes time to make a good picture and it doesn't seem too far-fetched to propose that, as Arbus begins to set up the shot, there is something about this man's gaze – how he looks at her from some far distance and yet, at the same time, seems as if he wants to take something from her – that reminds her of the time she and her brother, Howard, were fighting over a china doll. It was her doll, and she didn't know what he wanted with it, but he had tried to take it away (Howard claims not to remember any of this, now that they are grown up), and Arbus had held on tight, desperate to keep the thing, not because she liked it so much, but because it was being taken from her and she could not allow that. They had fought for a minute or more – Howard was stronger, but she would not be defeated – until, suddenly, the doll's porcelain head had shattered and one of the pieces had cut her – a deep cut, she still has the scar, and this is one of the reasons she loves Howard so much, because the marks of their childhood together are written on her body so that, even when he was trying to take something away from her, he had given her a kind of gift. A mark. A fleshly memory.

This man, though – this Avatar – is incapable of giving anything to anyone. Arbus had sensed that immediately. All he can do is take. Money, adoration, such love as his people have to offer – and even that isn't enough. Maybe the Family think he is giving them the community they have been searching for all their lives, maybe they believe that what he is taking from them is their sins, or the unspoken griefs of a half-lived existence, but the truth is that he wants every last thing they have, every scrap of hurt and smothered beauty and fright that they possess – the buried memories, the doll's broken mouth, the colour of the blood, the crescent-moon scar. He wants the minutiae of each life; he wants the details – because, after all, god is in the details, is he not? To be god, he has to look into the heart of everyone he meets and see every last detail – and that means he is something like her, because that is how she works. She has to see the inside, she has to find the telling detail in a face or a gesture. She has always worked like this, because there really are layers and layers of masks, the mask of what people think we want to see, the mask of what they would like to become, but after you get behind those masks, you have to penetrate further, to the naked yet strangely hopeful faces that are aware of being looked at and so transformed by the other's gaze. At times, the nature of this new transaction, this willingness to barter for hope and possibility and, at the last, the promise of some miraculous exposure, means that they are not so very different, she and this living god. And yet . . . *And yet* in every way that matters, they are opposites, she tells herself. Lyman is greedy, he wants everything and it can never be enough, so that he is as captivated by his followers as he is their object of adoration, whereas what drives her is curiosity, the hunger for a single, revealing detail, and all she needs is a moment, a glance, a word, some *tell* to let her in but also to release her again, the moment she is done. She doesn't want to stay. She doesn't want to captivate, or take possession – and what she fears, more than anything, what has almost happened so many more times than anyone else can be allowed to know, what terrifies her most is the possibility that she will lose control and stay too long. She will be trapped by some indecent impulse of pity or callow fellow feeling and lose herself. Mel Lyman will never lose himself: this living god is pitiless; that is what makes him a god. Or rather, that is what allows him to go on believing that he is a living deity, come in human form – though why a living deity should turn up in Fort Hill is anybody's guess.

No one is saying anything. When he looks at her, Lyman's face is a mask, and Arbus can't even tell if this is usual for him or a defence against revealing something that a god ought not to reveal. He has been sitting quietly, watching her, a blank expression on his face, and that hasn't bothered her at all, but now she is almost finished with the pretence of setting up. This was supposed to be an easy assignment but, all of a sudden, it all feels sad and ugly. There is nothing to see here, nothing to discover. She looks up at him. 'I used to read mottoes all the time,' she says. 'When I was a girl.' She fiddles with the light meter, using it as a prop to look at him without actually *looking* at him. 'On pennies, for instance,' she says. 'Where it says: *In God We Trust –* '

His expression doesn't change, but she senses amusement as he interrupts her. 'Is that a motto?' he says.

'Sure it is.'

'*In God We Trust?*'

'On pennies,' she says. 'When I was a little girl – '

He breaks in again, and he is still amused, but he isn't smiling. 'When was that?' he says quietly.

'When?'

'When were *you* a little girl?'

That surprises her, and she looks up at him again, without props, looking him in the eye. His face is impassive. There is nothing for the camera to reveal and yet, all at once, she feels that she is almost ready to take the picture, because *this* is what Lyman is. This is what makes him a god for those people. The impassiveness, the jab of a question with no emotion behind it and no curiosity, as if he were probing into the other's mind or heart or soul on behalf of the universe itself. A universe which is both divine and indifferent. She has the camera ready, but still it's not quite time, even though she is almost sure she knows what to do. 'During the Depression,' she says – but now, all of a sudden, she is tired again, tired and dulled in her mind and so very weary. This isn't an easy assignment, because it's not an assignment at all. There is nothing for the camera to find and that is the picture she is about to take: a photograph of that nothingness – and this is what they don't understand, the editors and agency people, an easy assignment is one that costs something, one where you have to charm or cajole or seduce the subject into revealing the one secret detail that nobody else ever sees. You have to give something of yourself to do that, but what they don't understand is that this is less tiring than giving and finding nothing. You have to give something of yourself but you also receive something in return, even if it's nothing more than an ordinary secret; and, now, what she was about to say runs through her head, unuttered: how, when she was a little girl during the Depression, she'd had a French governess who was very beautiful and very sad, and she had known that this woman, whom she loved more than her parents, was keeping a secret that she would never reveal to anyone – and that was what made people beautiful, that keeping of secrets. But this man she has been sent to photo-graph has no secrets to keep, he has made himself empty, so that anyone who chooses can see in his face whatever god they need – judge, father, enemy, lover, stranger, angel of healing, angel of regret. It doesn't matter what they come looking for, they find it here, because Mel Lyman is as empty as a mirror. If you aren't searching for some kind of god, though, there is nothing to see. Nothing at all.

Lyman is still looking at her, his face impassive. His question was intended to test her, no doubt, but it doesn't matter now and, after a brief, seemingly puzzled silence, the living god says something to the three girls in the corner and, slowly, with no obvious haste, they get up and leave the room. Even now, they act as if Arbus doesn't exist; they don't look at her, or say anything, they simply get up silently to leave and, when they are gone, the room feels dangerously empty. Mel Lyman tilts his head slightly. 'Are we waiting for someone?' he asks.

Arbus shakes her head. She doesn't like it, that he is looking at her; when she photographs people, she would rather they didn't look at her like this. It hadn't always been so – at one time, she would wait until the other person looked her in the eye – but now she thinks she will see them more clearly if they aren't watching her watching them. 'No,' she says, after a moment's pause. 'It's all ready now.'

GOOD FORTUNE

(P. J. Harvey, 2000)

Mid-July, 2013, another self-catered breakfast in a foreign town: Lipton Tea, soft-boiled eggs and buttered toast, the rain pouring down on the Dorfplatz outside, a good day for revenants and even if I can't imagine anyone coming from the afterlife on a day like this, to stand dripping outside my window, waiting to be let in, I feel them all out there, in their different ways, my mother who doesn't exist any more, taking form, yet again, as something else – a vine, a moth – and Christina, who is probably still alive somewhere, sleeping beside her husband in the suburb where they settled twenty years ago, for the good schools and the proximity to one or the other's place of work. A couple of years after I left Fulbourn, somebody told me Cathy was dead – just another suicide statistic, the glamour of her leaching away in some grimy bedsit – and over the years I've lost track of everyone else. After Christina, after I went mad and had to be locked away for my own good, I resolved to disappear, not by going off somewhere, but by being very still; as Ray Milland says, in his 1955 directorial debut, *A Man Alone*, 'a body doesn't have to get on a horse and ride a thousand miles to be running away', it's just as easy to stay put, to be still, to allow the good fortune of the details to take over. The sound of the rain. The smell of butter and lemons. The clouds forming over the roofs of this Alpine town. If I am missing someone, now, I don't know who she is, but there are several revenants to choose from and I can allow myself the tiny luxury of wishing one or the other of them was here, in the quiet confidence that nobody will show.

POSTLUDE: A NEW KIND OF LOVE

(Plants and Animals, 2008)

I am driving. It doesn't matter where, all that matters is that this is somewhere in America, I've got P. J. Harvey's *White Chalk* on the CD player and I've been driving all day. It was autumn this morning, and now it's winter, the cold sudden and decisive as evening draws in and I park the car, check into a hotel and head out to find somewhere to eat dinner. It's a pretty little town, the kind of town you think you could settle down in, for as long as you're passing through, just like the last pretty little town you passed through and I'm half expecting to hear Patti Page singing 'Tennessee Waltz' as I open the door to a place that looks like the kind of restaurant the locals might frequent, a place where the waitresses call you *Honey*, or *Darlin'*, and ask where you're from; but when I pass the bar and stand waiting to be seated beside a sign that says PLEASE WAIT HERE TO BE SEATED, I see that the place is half empty and remember that, for these people, it's late, dinner time comes early in these pretty little towns and the customers still at their tables are having coffee, leaving that decent interval after eating before they get up and go home to TV and an early night, because it's a weekday, and there's work in the morning for those who are fortunate enough still to have it.

So I'm waiting to be seated and taking the moment to snap out of the petty little hick-town cliché I've got going in my head when somebody comes over from the bar and touches me on the shoulder. I turn – and the woman who touched me, her hand still suspended in mid-air, backs away, so I think maybe I've been too abrupt, turning round, like maybe she thinks I'm annoyed or feel intruded upon and so, being British and all, I tell her I'm sorry. She seems puzzled by this, and I half expect her to say 'Sorry for what?' with that little upturn at the end of the sentence I've heard in these parts, but she doesn't say anything at all for a long moment and then, when she does speak, her voice sounds like the schoolteacher in *American Gothic*.

'Don't be sorry,' she says. 'I just wanted to let you know that they're done serving for the night.'

'Ah.' I don't have a watch, so I look around for a clock.

'It's nine thirty,' the woman says. 'Restaurant's closed, but you can still get something to eat from the bar.'

'Ah,' I say again; then, realising how stupid I must sound, I try to form a complete and more or less meaningful sentence. 'Do you – ?' My mind blanks. I had been about to ask if she worked here, but it's clear she's a customer, presumably at the bar, and I look over to see if there's someone waiting for her, some long-suffering boyfriend or work colleague, but there's no sign of anybody else at all, or nobody but a creased-looking guy in a baseball cap watching a basketball game on the TV. There's no barman even.

'Are you OK?' the woman asks.

She's twenty-five to thirty, very pretty, with a warm-toned, blue-eyed, sandy-blonde freshness about her that's about to tip me back into Clichéland at any moment, but now I have a question to focus on. 'I'm fine,' I say. 'It's just . . . I've been driving all day. I guess I didn't realise how tired I was.' Now I'm beginning to sound like the cliché. Maybe I've wandered into 'Twenty Four Hours from Tulsa' country. Not that this I anywhere near Tulsa.

She smiles. 'Well, you take a seat at the bar,' she says. 'Right over here by me. Sylvia will be right out.'

Many years ago, I had a job that took me on the road a good deal. My company always put me up in those mid-range corporate hotels that get routinely criticised for being bland and anonymous, but that was what I liked best about the traveller's life: the anonymity; the fact that, once I'd passed through the lobby and stepped into the elevator, I could be anywhere; the quiet of the room when I came in after a day of meetings, or a long drive, a quiet in which the day-long absence of me was almost palpable. The simple fact that nothing there was mine, so it was always like using somebody else's possessions. The glasses in the minibar. The TV remote. The soaps and body lotions. I could have been anyone.

It was such a pleasure not to be at home, to be away and living with the perennial possibility of disappearing altogether. That was a thought experiment that very quickly bordered on obsession: I would be in some foreign place – Madrid, say, or somewhere in Silicon Valley – and I would suddenly realise that there was nothing to prevent me hiring a car and driving for ten hours, or two days, until, finally, when I came to a place that felt right, I would rent a small apartment and move in, nothing to my name but the clothes I was wearing and the credit cards in my wallet. A fresh start, a new life; which is to say, a new life as someone else, a complete abandonment of the old self in favour of a life form that I had been carrying inside me for years, like a twin absorbed in the womb. A creature as yet undefined. An unknown quantity. Even at home, on a train journey of two or three hours, or on a short drive to a client's office, I saw myself disembarking at the wrong station, or taking a wrong turn, and moving into a two-up two-down house on a nondescript estate where nobody knew me. What I had in mind wasn't glamorous or exciting. If anything, it was very ordinary, very *quiet*: like the hush of a DIY store late on a Saturday afternoon when all the customers have left, or the low-level white noise of derelict industrial estates in the summer, dirty sunlight in the chain-link fences and kids squatting around bonfires, stoned on cheap wine and solvents.

This extended fantasy was an experiment in grey; what I was after was the world in monochrome. Once, when I still lived in Cowdenbeath, I had thought my first and second loves would happen in black and white. Winter events in that exhausted coal town where I grew up, halfway between the pithead and the old picture house, though not so far from the sea that I couldn't smell it sometimes through the ash and carbon. The picture house was my only church, and it provided most of my schooling. At the cheap matinees on Saturday afternoons I studied the vocabulary of monochrome: the gleam of snow on a back road to the

1900s; cat's-paws of light in a Viennese sewer, and black voices splashing away to what I was about to know as the Twentieth Century; the various incandescent deaths of Jimmy Cagney. I liked it when they ran the old black-and-white films, which they often did as they waited for the great epics to trickle down to us from the city; for reasons of my own, I didn't want too much colour back then, or not colour the way people had begun to see it after their eyes were infected with glorious Technicolor. I was as close to happy as I could imagine being, living in a town like mine, where the greys of the sky and the weather were so subtle, and you could spend hours gazing into a bonfire as it burned down to cinder and char, finding rare shades of grey and violet, of ash-pink and green and the pure, seared browns of scorched doornails. This was what I was after, as I disembarked from one plane and thought about checking in for another flight to somewhere nobody would think to look for me. I wanted the subtle extravagances of grey, the purer *richesse* of monochrome.

I had tried settling down. I'd moved into a semi-detached house in Commuterland, bought books about gardening and home entertaining, dug and top-dressed and planted shrubs from the local garden centre, baked puddings and foraged for chestnuts and blackberries in the surrounding countryside. I would come home with baskets full of plums from a tree I'd discovered in the ruins of a walled garden a couple of miles along the embankment, and I would sit at the kitchen table for hours, pricking the flesh with a needle to make my version of sloe gin. It was so like the home my mother had imagined for me long ago, when she still had hopes that I would become a professional person: the autumn woods, the heathland, the little villages strung out along the old railway line. Lunch in the gourmet pub with friends from the next village. Carol service at the local stately home, now owned by the National Trust. There was so much colour in the world but, like the photographs in interior-decorating magazines, it fell just short of convincing.

Nevertheless, I stayed for as long as I could. I tried hard to find a balance between the good life and the urge for going, but it was no use. I moved jobs, earned more money, stayed in better hotels, told myself my mother would be happy if she could see me now. Well, happy enough. I wasn't a doctor, or a lawyer, or a teacher in a college, but I had all the stuff she never had, the owner-occupier status and the performance bonuses. None of that worked, though: my unconscious, or my id, or the buried Narcissus of my absorbed twin – whatever name I give it, it's inexplicably there and beyond definition – that ghost self at the back of my mind started playing tricks on me. Mostly it was minor stuff, the psychopathology of everyday life: routine errors at work, hotel bookings cancelled for no reason, lapses in memory, lapses in judgement. Finally, the *coup de grâce* came – via the telephone network. Not just one telephone, but the entire system. It started at home but not long after it began following me about until, no matter where I was, I couldn't escape and, though there was nothing particularly sinister about the calls themselves, I knew someone or something was trying to get through to me. The pattern was simple: late at night, and sometimes first thing in the morning, the phone would ring but, when I picked it up, there was nobody there, just a faint noise that sounded like surf rolling on a shingle beach, far in the distance. Nothing else: just surf and shingle, and the obvious fact that this call was coming from some other time, carried to me through exchanges and relays that had ceased to exist decades ago. To begin with, I would ask this empty line over and over again who was calling; if I was in a hotel, I would call the front desk and demand that some embarrassed receptionist trace my last caller. It was no good, though, and after a while I stopped talking and listened to that sound, waves, shingle, and now and then what I thought was like a bird call. Sometimes I just lifted the receiver, then set it back without even putting it to my ear, but usually I would listen for a while before I hung up. After a few weeks of this, I began to understand that the calls weren't real, that they had to be hallucinations – auditory hallucinations of distance, surf, a faraway beach – but the ringing of the phone was so lifelike, and even at my most rational, even when I assured myself that this was just a symptom of stress, or fatigue, I kept on listening for that voice through the sound of the waves, a voice I had taken for a bird call, but eventually concluded was something else, something like my own voice, calling from a pit town in the snow, trying to tell my future self, through a decades-long wash of static and monochrome, that everything had to change.

Though the evening is not as young as it was, Selena and I aren't moving. We've settled into our own warm zone, eye contact, lingering conversation, a kind of golden, protective light around where we are sitting. It's been just the two of us since the baseball cap got up, paid his tab and wandered off into the night mumbling what I assumed was a goodbye, and now it's snowing outside, a soft, slow snow that will soon begin to settle. I should be getting back to my hotel, but we are in the middle of a conversation; I don't feel tired any more, and the beer is good, some local microbrewery IPA that I've never heard of and will most likely never taste again. These are the details that beglamour us on this kind of one-night – what? Flirtation? Romance? I don't want to classify it, I'm just going along, not expecting anything, because I really like this woman – who isn't a schoolteacher, but coincidentally *is* called Selena which, when she said it, recalled the name of the character she sounds like in *American Gothic*, the sultry schoolteacher who has a thing going with the town sheriff, who may or may not be The Devil Himself. *Selena Coombs*. That was her name. Selena Coombs, played, as I recall, by Brenda Bakke. Only this Selena, the Selena who isn't a schoolteacher and looks more Laura Dern than Brenda Bakke, isn't a Coombs, she's a Warren, the daughter, I have recently learned, of someone called Jim Warren, a real estate developer and entrepreneur who owns, among other things, the hotel where I am staying, though I have no immediate plan to go back there and get the decent night's sleep I so obviously need. I'm not sure why the daughter of what might be the richest man in town is sitting in this cosy-but-basic little bar drinking beer with me, but I do know that we are playing a game, and I don't want that game to stop.

It's a game I have played all my life, and I'm still an incompetent, but I'm not so bad at it that I don't know my ineptitude is part of the charm, at least where someone like Selena Warren is concerned. I have spent over three decades unconsciously learning to read signs, to interpret body language, to respond, still unconsciously, in measured and appropriate ways, to avoid seeming needy, on the one hand, and cold on the other. I like the game, mostly because I don't think of it as having an outcome, but it's usually my random partner who adds the modicum of grace that makes it so enjoyable. I'm always a step behind – but then, this is the part I most enjoy, so I don't mind if it gets a little drawn out and, apparently, Selena doesn't mind either. In fact, for now at least, she seems happy, or at least pleasantly diverted. She is very attractive, even beautiful in this light, and the way she plays the game suggests a certain openness to things going either way, a no-strings, in-the-moment spirit that isn't anywhere near as common as it might be. I like playing along with her. However, the pleasant, rather plain woman who brought food and beer earlier appears to have disappeared altogether, and it's starting to look like closing-up time. I'm not anxious, or not yet, but I know this game has an end, it has a *goal*, even, a point at which an agreement is reached and a line crossed. A glancing touch, a kiss, a look. A commitment, or the start of one that, for all anyone knows, is the first in a series of possible commitments, leading who knows where.

I also know that this end point can be precipitated by some outside circumstance: closing time, for instance. The trouble is, I don't actually want to take this game any further than where it is now. I want to sit and talk all night, with the snow brushing the windows and forming in white drifts on the street outside, but I don't want to move to some next stage. I like what's happening now. Once, my Aunt Margaret said, apropos of nothing: I believe in long engagements – and I recall how thrilled my child self was by that notion. To draw things out, to play the game; to defer, though never quite refuse; to choose, by mutual agreement, not to commit. That's what I want right

now: I want *this* moment to last. I don't want to go home with
Selena and drink wine in a lamplit kitchen. I don't want to kiss
her; I don't want to undress her; I don't want to make love to
her – and I don't want to wake up to an array of dolls or stuffed
toys gazing vacantly at me from a dressing table or a newly
reupholstered chesterfield. I don't want to be alone with her and
it's not impossible that I might not want to be alone with anyone
ever again. I know that story and, these days, I don't care how
it ends. I'm still the fool I always was and it can take no more
than a look or a gesture, or even a shift in the register of a
stranger's voice, to put a spell on me, but afterwards I would
only want to drive away and lie down in my motel cabin,
listening to the owls or the coyotes or whatever else is out there
in the dark. Out in the dark, where, as I still imagine it, my
real love is driving home with the windows open on a hot
Midwestern night, or sitting in a college library reading *Nine
Stories* by J. D. Salinger, a book she has read many times. This
is not Christina, by which I mean this is not the historical
Christina, the woman who was once twenty and is now fifty-
five; this is someone else, this is the other to my other. Not an
Echo, never a reflection, this is the one who reminds me that
the other is beautiful, simply by being, fully and wilfully, *other*
– which is not the same thing as joining in with the chorus on
some Everything-is-Beautiful pop-Christian mantra à la Ray
Stevens,[34] because for a good part of the time, we are not being
other, we're being the *us* that we were taught to be, the *us* for

---

[34] A chart-topping single for Stevens in 1970, my mother loved the B-side
'A Brighter Day'.

which, from now and then, someone will sacrifice all judgement, or independence, or pride, and end up scrawling bloody graffiti on the doors of a house where everyone inside is dead, or drinking down the poison the way you were taught in Jonestown.

'Loneliness,' Mel Lyman says, 'is the sole motivation, the force that keeps man striving after the unattainable, the loneliness of man separated from his soul, man crying out into the void for God, man eternally seeking more of himself through every activity, filling that devouring need on whatever level the spirit is feeding, the arena of conflict, be it flesh, thoughts, aspiring to ideals, man searches for love to satisfy his gaping hunger.' Dodgy rhetoric aside, he may be right, but every con man who knows what he's about can smell the needy and the hungry a mile off; go down to the dark end of the fair, or the dark end of the street for that matter, and you'll see: it happens every night and, more often than not, the soul learns the cost of belonging the hard way, whether we're talking about community, transgression or romantic love. But why belong at all? Or rather, why belong according to rules based on family and church and social hierarchies? Why have the set-in-stone fixity of church when there is the constant flicker and flow of gospel, written, as it is, on the wind, hard to decipher but joyous in the apprehension? Why would anyone think that love, or, for that matter, life itself, has to be *everlasting*?

I don't want to go home with Selena; though, of course, I don't want her to know that either. I don't want her to know that I could sit here and talk all night, but when it comes time to go, I want to go alone – and she clearly senses that something is going on with me because she lays her hand on my arm and leans closer. 'You're tired,' she says. 'You've had a long day – '

I shake my head. I don't want to stop, even if I don't want to go any further. I just want to stay here. 'No, really . . .' I begin – and then I look at her, at her blue eyes and her mouth, which I suddenly wish I could kiss, before I hurry out the door and away, not back to my own life, but to the next morning, the next drive, the anonymity of the road – and in the turn of a moment I see, not only that she has understood how I felt all along, that, in fact, she knew how I felt even before I did, but also that she feels the same way. It's a good notion, and I don't have any difficulty believing that, even if we did start out on the usual weekday-night flirtation, we felt sure from the beginning that we weren't going to slide into the usual script, because we'd sensed something in each other that could have been taken for reticence, but isn't, quite. We'd sensed a new kind of love, a nascent preparedness for something else, a preparedness that, for all either of us knew, might never end – and it has to be said that, after the usual formalities, we left one another with good grace that night, with good grace and, on my part at least, more than a little wistfulness for what we were both refusing – and, if I am wholly honest, I have to admit that, once I'd understood that she intended going home alone, that wistfulness shaded into something like regret, and it was a long time before I stopped thinking about her mouth and went to sleep. Though, for all anyone knows, she might have felt that way too, and just as deeply. As soon as we parted – with a warm, collegiate, slightly extended hug outside the restaurant in the falling snow – I was wishing I had kissed her, just once. But then, there was the pleasure of afterwards to be lingered over, the pleasure of crossing a street in the same snow, then turning a corner and walking the length of the next street, snow forming on my hair and coat, to where the hotel was, walking by the light of the street lamps and falling back on what people fall back on at that time of the morning. A Marvin Gaye song at the back of the mind, or a scene from an old movie you love so much and know so well, it feels like a personal memory. That night, for me, it was the corniest fallback of all: a Sufi parable that, for reasons nobody with any sense would disclose, I once got off by heart:

A lover came to the dwelling of the Beloved and asked to be admitted.

'Who is there?' the Beloved asked.

'I am here,' the lover answered. But the Beloved refused to admit the lover.

After wandering in grief and longing for many long years, the lover returned to the Beloved and begged once again to be admitted.

'Who is there?' asked the Beloved.

'You alone are there,' the lover answered.

And the door opened.

CODA: (IT'S THE) SAME OLD SONG

(*The Four Tops, 1965*)

Insomnia is the most beautiful of our afflictions. Cruel, admittedly; but then, cruelty and beauty are closer kin than we usually choose to imagine. Without insomnia, I would never find myself in the yard at two in the morning, chopping wood for the stove by the light of a winter moon. Without insomnia, I would never have driven thousands of hours across prairie or up and down coast roads in the dark, the world turning to *film noir* around me, every lit house and roadside Steak 'n Shake a local theatre of dimming gold and everyday mystery. Without insomnia, I wouldn't have learned how the Four Tops' 1965 hit, 'It's the Same Old Song', got its title ('Duke' Fakir tells the story to Peter Sagal on an episode of NPR's *Not My Job*, broadcast on 21 January 2012). None of this matters to anybody else, I know, but insomnia informs the texture and gravity of my days as well as my nights, because insomnia is where the secrets and half-memories come up into the half-light to feed, and I catch glimpses of the life I might have had, a life that, for a few hours, resembles a scene from a movie – or rather, the way a scene from a movie resembles life as it must be lived in some other place by our more graceful selves, which is to

257

say, by the people we would have been, had we been more *thrawn*, more attuned to *glamourie* and the romance of the land and, so, more committed to the overall narrative.

Like late-night television and certain species of roadside diner (going to a Steak 'n Shake[35] in the daytime is having a meal, but stopping by at three in the AM is something else), I suspect that the Internet was created for insomniacs, by insomniacs – and it must have been around about three in the morning on yet another sleepless night when I found a picture of Christina on her home business website. Back in the 1970s, when I met and lost her, a friend said she was the most beautiful girl he had ever seen and if I close my eyes I can picture her now: incandescently beautiful, and very young. Yet as young as she was, she could see right through anyone who tried to deceive her, just as she saw through all my lies of omission. That night, from the photograph of herself that she had put up on her website, I could see that she was still beautiful, but she wasn't a girl any more, and I thought I detected in her face a history of having seen through too many deceptions. Naturally, I could be wrong in this – at three in the morning, after several days of little or no sleep, the back of the mind shuffles on according to its own, often perverse logic – and I saw that, if I really wanted

[35] 'Famous for Steak 'n Shake Steakburgers. In 1934, in Normal, Illinois, Steak 'n Shake started grilling real-steak STEAKBURGER™ sandwiches, hand-dipping real-milk Milk Shakes and serving them to your table on real china. Nowadays, in over 430 restaurants in 20 states, we're still cooking STEAKBURGER™ patties to order, along with a full menu of other favorites, same as we always have. And because we're open 24 hours a day, you can stop by anytime.' (*Extract from the company website*)

to, I had the means to find out how she was now and perhaps make amends in some way for my behaviour over three decades ago. Now, I could finally answer her last letter by simply typing the words into my computer and emailing them to the address on the Contact page and, of course, I resolved to do exactly that, very soon. Very soon, though not right away. I have learned much less in my life than I expected to learn, but I do know that you shouldn't write emails to *anyone* at three o'clock in the morning.

It's a cliché, of course, to say that a whole life can turn on a word, or a gesture; it's another thing altogether to remember so vividly how it happened and to recall, too late, what Pound says in Canto 81:

> Here error is all in the not done,
> all in the diffidence that faltered . . .

Not that it matters, now, to anyone other than my hidden twin, the *thrawn* Jungle Creep deep inside the cradle of my flesh, yearning to throw off the burden of my errors, my sins, my ordinary and unforgivable cowardice.

The first time I saw Jean-Gabriel Albicocco's film of *Le Grand Meaulnes*, I was at the cinema club in a Belgian seaside town. There were around twenty other people in the room, not a cinema, but a school assembly hall with a portable screen just in front of the stage and ten rows of stacking chairs set out neatly by a janitor in a grey work coat that he never took off, in spite of the fact that it was high summer, and the hall was hot and airless. At the time, I didn't really know what was going on: the film was in French, with Flemish subtitles, and I didn't know enough of either language to follow the dialogue. Or not to begin with, at least. When the boys are in school, and the big, awkward Meaulnes arrives, gawky and other-worldly in clothes that aren't right for him, I couldn't understand a word of what anyone was saying, and I felt awkward and other-worldly myself, sitting in an audience of native speakers, and so present at this viewing under something like false pretences – because I *had* pretended to be what I was not, mumbling a greeting in bad French to the person at the door, an oddly handsome boy in spite of his pimples and the striped tank top he wore over a grey polyester shirt. I quickly handed over my entry money, which I had counted out beforehand to avoid a lengthy transaction, then took my seat. I had a foolish, or perhaps superstitious, idea that if the people in the film club knew how flimsy my grasp of their language was, they would think of me as an interloper, like a stranger at a country wedding. I didn't mind if the oddly handsome boy thought I was a foreigner: he might imagine I was a student at the local college, or a youngish-looking visitor from the university town further south: foreign, without a doubt, but sufficiently francophone, or Flemish-speaking, to follow a movie that was, in itself, fairly complicated.

I was none of these things, however, and for the first forty minutes the film was a strangely painful experience, an exercise, not so much in frustration or bewilderment as in a quite illogical, but truly excruciating, fear. Excruciating: the very origin of the word is odd, yet it's the perfect descriptive term for the more or less religious experience I had that evening. I had no particular attachment to the story – I hadn't even read the book – and no particular motive in going besides the relative pleasure of passing the time at a film show rather than wandering the streets of what was otherwise rather a dull town, where people came from far and wide, it seemed, to eat chips dunked in mayonnaise, drink strong beer and listen to jollified medleys of popular fifties songs arranged for the Hammond organ, or for a tenor saxophone that was utterly unaware of jazz. In short, I was a footloose youth looking for something to do and, having seen a flyer advertising the movie in French that even I could understand, I'd gone along. I had no vested interest in this film and I'd never heard of Albicocco, or even Alain-Fournier for that matter. Yet almost immediately, certainly after the first few scenes, I was filled with a sense of almost unbearable urgency, a need to know not just the general terms of the narrative, but every detail, every nuance, every allusion. I wanted to know the film's religious core, its litany of saints, its theodicy; I needed to understand its secret, possibly anarchic politics. These people were utterly mysterious to me – and yet, at the same time, I felt as if I were watching a possible version of my own life, unfolding before me in a language I barely knew, with nothing to help me but a series of distracting subtitles in a language I didn't know at all. Which should, I suppose, have been nothing more than a mild irritation, a self-imposed trial that any idle traveller might fall into on a quiet, overcast evening in a foreign town. What I felt, however, was a sudden fear, a *horror* of my own condition that I could neither explain nor evade, sitting there in the fourth row, transfixed, unable to get up and walk out, so fascinated was I by the mystery of the *autremonde* that was claiming me – or rather, darkly glamouring me – from that slightly lopsided portable screen.

It is possible that, on any other day, or in any other mood than the mood I was in that evening, I would have left that assembly hall with nothing more than a crush on Juliette Villard[36] and a resolution to improve my French (in the event that I should one day meet her – in Nantes, say, or on a train to Marseille); certainly, I find myself unable to explain that initial fear, that horror of having been put in the wrong body, at the wrong place and time, just as I cannot explain, and admit to being mildly embarrassed by, the sudden, possibly visible joy I felt when Meaulnes finds the lost world. All at once, the fear dissolved, my mind was emptied of thought and I understood, not in the usual way of working out the story, but physically, in my blood and in my bones, what it meant to pass from a dark childhood into a world so genuinely rich that it is beyond beautiful, because it is already lost even as we enter it. I was filled with light and colour, my mind and body illumined by an intuition of what it meant to be alive in the fullest sense and in pursuit of an impossible prize, a pursuit whose inevitable failure is neither here nor there for as long as the story is being told. From that moment on, the film *had* me; what happened next was infinitely more important than anything that was happening in my own day-to-day existence and, though I felt confident that it would end in romantic, rather than sentimental mode, I waited anxiously for the final scene, only relaxing when it became clear that Meaulnes

[36] Juliette Villard was born on Halloween 1942, and died in Paris on 16 March 1971. She is buried at the Château-Gombert cemetery in Marseille, directly opposite the tomb of Simone Simon, who starred in Jacques Tourneur's unforgettable *Cat People* in 1942.

will abandon the beautiful girl he met in the lost world – why I wasn't sure, though it seemed to have something to do with Juliette Villard's character. In retrospect, having watched the film several times since, I have to confess that it does tend towards the sentimental, but that doesn't matter now. What matters is what happened that one evening in a grey Flemish town and, though it matters only to me, and to nobody else, that was the evening when I first understood that *glamourie* is more beautiful, and certainly more dangerous, than any other story we can tell because nobody can be glamoured from this world, the source has to come from some other place: from *l'autremonde*, from fairy time, from the other side of the looking glass. To be glamoured I have to feel that 'I dwell in Possibility, a fairer house than Prose' (as Emily Dickinson says), but with that under-standing comes the sad, though not sentimental, realisation that *glamourie* cannot last – that, to be permanent, it has to be able to sustain itself in this world, a world only very occasionally unprosaic. It may well be a stray thread of eternity, but fairy time isn't permanent and, no matter how much he might love Beatrice, Dante has to live with Mrs Alighieri, a woman named Gemma with whom he had several children, though he never once mentions her in his poems.

With insomnia there comes a different kind of winter life, cold, frost-hard, almost without scent, so that anything – a snuffed candle, an orange, new bread – any given thing is implausibly rich and sweet, and the least glancing touch becomes a ripple of event, like the paths formed in magnetised iron. When it gets to this point in the turning of the year, I like to tend the stove in the far end of the house, away from where the others are sleeping. It is a pleasurable and unnecessary task, to fill it with logs and watch it burn, and after a while – it varies from night to night, but sooner or later – this ordinary task of tending the fire, alone and finally quiet, begins to feel like an arrival. A belonging. Perhaps it wasn't always so, but now, watching the flames take, I feel myself coming in, the way an oceangoing boat comes in to harbour, slowly, piloted by the ordinary facts of another night. There is no reason to think this feeling will last – for the most part, nature is averse to steady states – but for an hour at a time it can feel like the future I told myself would come long ago, a future I used to imagine as a hurt, unhappy child, sitting up on my windowsill at Blackburn Drive, listening to the owls in Kirk's woods, a storybook latter days that I would lay out in my mind again when I was in the asylum, making sense of it and putting it all together like the pieces of a jigsaw, till it became, not a picture so much as an atmosphere, something dark and sweet like the mist that films the glass in a child's bedroom, or that early-morning absence in the snow where unknown animals have left their traces in the dark while the house was sleeping. When I need more wood, I go out to the yard, hoping I might see a fleet body hurrying away, and sometimes I do, but mostly I split a few logs and go back inside, carrying the cold on my skin like a charm. This is where the body seems truest, where it seems most creaturely, but I have no idea what the local fauna makes of me – and the same questions come up every time, in more or less the same form. Do I belong here? Do any of us belong on this earth any more? Who among us knows what confusion we create when we step outside in the dark and the scents from our bodies, scents tinged with soap and garlic and smoke, drift into the woods or the desert beyond our fence lines? We live inside a *grimoire* we cannot read, wet musks along our borderlines, pheromone trails in a dew-sodden lawn, the almost faecal aroma of a subtropical night – and we write, in that same book, random and possibly unintelligible graffiti across the pages.

Or so I think. But when I go back inside, my mind falls quiet again and, as I settle by the stove, that sense of belonging returns, which is to say a belonging that is not to this or any specific place, or to any community or faction or tribe, but to the dust from which I came and to which my body will return, and to the entire corpus of the creaturely. Spring tide and chert and blizzard. Flamingo and bobolink and pine. The lives of unknown others who are awake in the dark, watching fires, or writing in tattered notebooks like this one. That I live in this house is neither here nor there: as Robert Burton says, 'All places are distant from heaven alike, the sun shines happily as warm in one city as in another, and to a wise man there is no difference of climes; friends are everywhere to him that behaves himself well, and a prophet is not esteemed in his own country.' What matters is to recognise that the great romance is the land itself. Or rather: the great romance is that intersection between time and place that we so casually refer to as 'the moment'. That moment, that experience of time, is the Beloved of old tales. The human beloved, however cherished he or she may be, is there to bear shared witness to that now, to act as a fellow celebrant, significant because they see that moment in its full glamour. We may belong to a lover, or a Family, or some version of community for a while, but we belong for all time to the land, which is to say, to gravity, to individual perishability and to the society of other creatures – and because none of these specific instances lasts, everything endures.

Besides, how can I tell myself that I belong here in some exclusive way when suddenly, in my mind's eye, I am walking a long, deserted road in northern Indiana. It's 1997, mid-October, late afternoon in the woods and everything smells a little of sugar, one last wisp of summer's lease before the return of the frost. I've arrived at this place by way of a series of those straggling towns and settlements that congeal around road crossings, or places where trains used to stop, the land about them wide and apparently empty – and from here, it seems, I have no destination. By slow degrees, while I was looking the other way, late afternoon in the woods has turned to evening on the road and more snow is certain, yet even though the lights of the farmsteads and restaurants look so very appealing, I have a sense that the inside isn't quite as *heimlich* as it's cracked up to be and I keep on walking. The inside has rules, it has people who know where they belong – and while I don't agree with Sartre that hell is others, people who know where they belong can be a definite inconvenience. Choosing to remain outside is the most graceful of refusals and, having come to this point, it seems that the only grievous error would be to allow oneself to be lured back into the entire apparatus of property values and marital status and ballot papers. What better alternative than to be the wanderer, like Augustin Meaulnes, or Narcissus for that matter, perpetually vanishing into a lost domain, which is both the only place that cannot be colonised by the rules and, at the same time, the territory where we meet the true others, the ones who are here only in passing, or by chance, looking for lost domains of their own, in the changing light, or at the dark end of the fair?[37]

I remember standing by the river with Christina that summer night, the pull of the water echoing in my body, a gravity I knew, not from what I'd read in schoolbooks, not from the thought in Newton's head the day he saw the apple fall, but from the tug and sway of it, the magnetic tide that makes us what we sense ourselves to be when we're unseen, the barely conscious sense of something hidden, shifting as we drift along a towpath at nightfall, a breath away and *possible* in a way nothing else has been for years. I wish I'd known back then that it wasn't *us* I loved, but something abroad on the meadows, a swim of warmth that held us for an instant, as it flowed from here to there, the way the sun swims across a mile of ripening wheat then darkens in the local sway of matter. The cattle watched from the other bank, included in the gravity we made as I stood helpless, unable to see that *I* wasn't the drama, *I* wasn't the story – it was everything: the cattle, the river, Christina, me, we were all included in that same gravity. Why I couldn't see that, I do not know, but if I had, I might have pulled down my vanity and accepted what I was being offered. Or maybe I could have found a way to explain that my refusal was not – or not only – a symptom of ordinary

[37] ''Twas this on tables I had seen / When turning, hungry, lone, / I looked in windows, for the wealth / I could not hope to own.' (Emily Dickinson)

fear, some Freudian perversity, or Catholic guilt trip, or the old clichéd madonna–whore thing but rather, that it was a compliment of sorts, and for that matter, a compliment on the highest level. A compliment because it acknowledged from the outset that, in our particular case, the options offered by the outside world were all of them beneath us, at the moment, and that I could not bear to collaborate with some descent into the banal that might have one of us repeating, after one too many drinks, Ambrose Bierce's old definition, *Love: a temporary insanity curable by marriage.* Maybe it's only the insomnia talking, but at the back of my mind, there's a scenario where she understands, at some point in her own account of that summer, that I loved her more than I had ever imagined possible, and so, as confused and foolish and cruel as I was at the time, the fact remained that, this world being what it is, I had no choice but to walk away.

No memory happens in the past. To say this in so many words is, no doubt, to state the obvious – our memories happen now, in the madeleine- and tisane-tinctured present – but it strikes me as peculiar, still, that my recollections have so little to do with historical time. When I recall a golden or terrifying after-noon from my childhood, when the name of an old friend suddenly crops up in one of those private conversations I have with myself while driving or soaking in the bathtub, I rarely have a specific day, or a specific year, in mind. All the summers of childhood are distilled to one afternoon and everything that ever happened in sunlight or June rain happened on that one day. All the Christmases of my blithe teens take place in the space of one snow-lit and vaguely clandestine winter and the only clue to external time, the time of calendars and TV documentaries, is that almost every event that happens in this infinite now is tagged with a phrase from a song, something by Elvis, say, or the Four Tops – and because this is so, all the women I have ever known are also Christina.

It may appear that, after due consideration, this sounds wrong – and for a long time I also subscribed to the cod-psychoanalytical orthodoxy that every affair I had in my life was, one way or another, an echo of my relationship with my mother. That old cliché. It turns out, though, that a different, if not altogether opposite, condition applies: my mother was the first instance of a figure I would search for over and over until Christina appeared, and I came to understand that every woman I had ever known was an approximation of that genus type. The French teacher I had a crush on, aged twelve. The young German woman I met at the Eagle who, in a certain, alcohol-tinged light, resembled Kim Novak. The girl I danced with all evening at the Catholic Club disco then didn't ask out and never spoke to again, walking away in the rain out of stubborn and inexplicable perversity, just as I would walk away later, and keep walking, not once, but as often as it took to refuse what I most longed for. All the holiday romances and the women I tried to live with, in and out of love or never in love in the first place and too shy to say so, all the beautiful girls and women I ever passed in the street in Paris or Kiev or Buenos Aires, even my cousin Madeleine and, yes, my mother too – they were all forms of Christina. The paradox, however, is that now I have come to understand this, I also understand that Christina herself has become, and perhaps always was, a fiction.

Another song my mother used to sing was Vera Lynn's wartime weepie, 'We'll Meet Again'. As a teenager, I dismissed that song (and her), because I didn't understand the need to reinhabit the clichés and so reclaim the underlying truths they obscured. I was too clever for that. Now, I only have to sit still in my chair and I can hear her singing along with the radio – *We'll meet again, don't know where, don't know when* – and I want to lie down on the floor and weep because I have come to realise that she knew what a burden her love was, and how much tact and self-restraint she exercised in a vain attempt not to overwhelm me with it. I remember her smiling, as she showed me the photograph of my father, smiling at how surprised I was and, at the same time, smiling to cover up the fear she had already begun to nurture, not so far in the back of her mind as it ought to have been, that I would turn out to be him. *Don't tell your father*, she had said – but then, she said that often, in trivial matters and great. Don't tell your father, he wouldn't understand. Or was it that he would understand all too well, and who knew what that understanding would cost us?

I didn't make that call to Christina. Of course I didn't. It took only a few minutes of daylight thinking to see that the person I had missed for so long, the person I had sworn to find again, without ever making the least effort to do so, was over thirty years gone. I sat for a long time staring at that stranger on my computer screen, but I couldn't connect her with the twenty-two-year-old I had loved and refused and, in the end, I had to switch off the machine and go back to my wood-burning stove, with nothing more to show for my chance discovery than a handful of memories that I could no longer trust, because I had spent so much time, first rewriting, and then attempting to erase them. Maybe that is the real problem with insomnia: it allows the mind too much time. Time to second-guess, time to rebuild what was never there in the first place.

We'll meet again. Yes, but not as *us*. Because *we* is larger than *us*. *We* is the whole story, the infinite game; *us* is just local chapter and verse. It's the same old song and I know we'll meet again. I know we'll meet again, but then life is bigger, bigger than you and you are not me, bigger than us and the mystery endlessly deepens and we part again, not having said what we wanted to say, not having done what we should have done, but any suspicion of futility that we may entertain here is both foolish and impudent. It's the same old song; yes, and it's always changing. And I know we'll meet again, don't know where, don't know when. It might be a sunny day, it might not, but there's a place for us, somewhere, and we'll go on meeting, in every possible form and, if we're lucky, we'll glamour one another with grace and tenderness. Sometimes this will feel like love, more often it will be a glance or a word in passing, worldly circumstances, or some inexplicable hesitation holding us back, but there's a beauty in this as well. Maybe that sounds like a sentimentalist talking, I don't know, but I do know that if it is, then the romantic is never very far behind to say, yes, we'll meet again, yes, it's inevitable, mother and child, lover and lover, father and son. We'll meet again. Over and over and over, we will always meet again. Though not as *us*.

ACKNOWLEDGEMENTS

'I Put a Spell on You', 'Sixth Digression: Why Being Lost Is An Instance Of Good Fortune' and 'Seventh Digression: On the Mountains of the Moon' were first published in the *London Review of Books*.

'Second Digression: On *Thrawn*' was commissioned by *La Nouvelle Revue Française* and published in March 2012 in a translation by Stephane Audéguy.